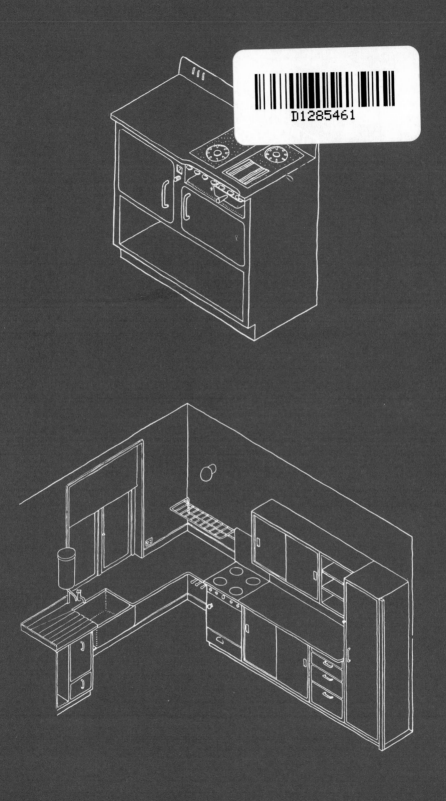

THIS BOOK IS DEDICATED TO MY FATHER,
GRANT HAYWARD

THE MODERN KITCHEN

TIM HAYWARD

Photography by Sarah Hogan

quadrille

Prestige

egg beater

Prestige
Sky-line
FOREIGN

PYREX
tumbler
with BLUE holder

for both hot and cold drinks

A 'COLE & MASON' SPICE
LONDON-ENGLAND.
MODEL 157 6 COLOUR

LE CREUSET

SERVICE A FONDUE

COMPLETE SAFETY

• Fondue forks (6)
integral handles
(made in Thiers, France)

• Pot :
cast iron enamelware
perfect stability

• Burner : high precision
liquid alcohol stainless
steel burner.

Réf. 6001

SECURITE TOTALE

LE CREUSET

habitat

fondue

CONTENTS

INTRODUCTION

Today, we regard the kitchen as the heart of our home. It's where we get together as families, where we do the daily work of feeding ourselves and those we love. Yet the kitchen in a modern Western house is a bizarre hybrid – part leisure space, part work space – simultaneously a room and, when 'fitted' with a unique combination of furniture, trimmings and appliances, a single, desirable 'consumer durable'. The average UK family spends more on a new kitchen than they do on a car or holiday.* Until we went crazy about weddings it was the biggest expenditure after the house itself.

There is nowhere in daily domestic life where design impinges quite as much as in the kitchen – where Le Corbusier's dictum that the home should be 'a machine for living',† or Louis H. Sullivan's observation that 'form ever follows function',‡ are more in evidence. In a society that largely rejected modernism in architecture, the appliances, the furniture, the kitchen itself are the surviving exemplars of the philosophy: design with a practical rigour that cuts through any amount of romantic nostalgia.

It's a fair argument that the kitchen was invented the moment mankind had tamed fire sufficiently to bring it indoors. Cooking on the home hearth is the same in a reindeer-skin tent far above the Arctic Circle, an earth-floored shelter in Equatorial Africa, and pretty much everything in between.

All most of us know of traditional kitchens comes from two sources: cookbooks and the heritage industry. Right up until the 20th century cookbooks lived not in the kitchen with the cooks, but in the libraries of masters and mistresses, used for the 'guidance' of often illiterate staff. Surviving examples of working kitchens are almost universally those in the great houses that we now treat as museums. For the aristocracy and most of the middle class, 'cooking' meant the work done in kitchens staffed by servants. This was the section of society with surplus wealth, who could make choices about food and eating. They ate good food but, in accordance with rigid social convention, rarely entered the place where it was prepared.

For me, the story of the modern kitchen begins as servants disappear and as working people attain the means to own and equip their own kitchens. It is not perhaps a meaningful idea in the historical or anthropological sense, but for me it's when 'ordinary people' enter kitchens and set about the business of cooking that the space starts to become interesting.

---

* In the most recent edition of *The Housebuilder's Bible* it is recommended to budget around £11,400 ($15,000) to equip a domestic kitchen (this figure can obviously go up or down depending on quality). Although some of this figure can be explained by spend on appliances, much of it is taken up with the aptly named 'units' – the fibreboard set-dressing from a single supplier or designer that makes up the modern 'fitted kitchen'.

† From Le Corbusier's 1923 manifesto, *Vers Une Architecture* (*Toward An Architecture*).

‡ From Sullivan's 1896 essay, 'The Tall Office Building Artistically Considered'.

For most of us our kitchens and the objects in them are the definition of 'quotidian' – so ordinary that they seem insignificant and near-invisible. But objects so very close to us are the ones best evolved to our lives and most reflective of them. Every object has a design history; some manufactured objects have corporate 'origin myths'. All are worthy of attention. After all, if everyday objects cannot tell powerful stories, why do we have museums?

At the moment there is little research into or study of the modern kitchen and this book is by no means a comprehensive history – but it's a start.

I'm a little more obsessive about kitchens than most. For me it's not just where I cook and eat with my family, but also a place of work – a study, laboratory and studio. Part of the reason I love spending time in it is that every single object is selected and placed carefully and daily judged for its utility. If a single one fails, I am ruthless in editing it out. The kitchen is a constantly mutating expression of self – and I suspect this is more than a little true of everyone. The home kitchen, its layout, set-up and selection of kit, has always been a surprisingly neat illustration of our beliefs, tastes, aesthetics and aspirations – simultaneously the heart of our homes and a vivid snapshot of our domestic lives.

PREPARATION

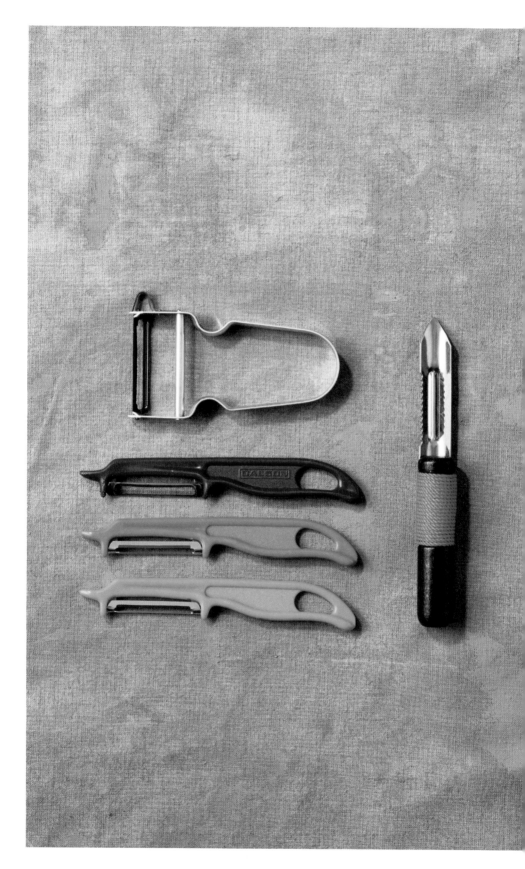

POTATO PEELER

YOU CAN PEEL a vegetable with any old knife, but it takes skill to remove only the thinnest layer so as not to waste the good stuff underneath. The vegetable or potato peeler means that even a relatively unskilled cook can do a good job quickly and safely. The principle is simple: the blade is protected by a guard, which also controls the depth to which it cuts, not unlike a safety razor. In effect, the peeler renders what is often the sharpest blade in the domestic kitchen safe and user-friendly.

The traditional pattern in the UK is for the blade to be in a straight line with the handle. It's held in exactly the same way as a paring knife, with the fingers wrapped round the handle, pulling the blade back toward the thumb. There are a variety of designs, but the favourite is known as a 'Lancashire' peeler, easily recognisable by the orange string holding the blade to the handle (*opposite, far right*). Most have a point for digging out eyes or rotten spots from the potato, but some have a tubular tip designed for coring apples. Because only one side of the blade slot is sharpened, traditional peelers were often inconvenient for left-handers to use and special versions were made by some companies.

The 'Rex' peeler was launched by the Zena company in Switzerland in 1947 and has remained unchanged ever since (*centre, top*). It's a ruthlessly efficient piece of kit with a skeletal aluminium handle and a ferociously sharp steel blade positioned at 90 degrees to it. Because the peeler blade can't be sharpened, most types need to be replaced regularly, but for some reason the Rex type seems to go on forever, even when used to shave Parmesan or chocolate.

The Rex, often referred to by chefs as the 'speed peeler', is used with the vegetable held in one hand and the tool held in the other with a sort of whittling action. The Rex cuts both ways and is ambidextrous by design. The sharp 'eye-gouger' is made of the same blued steel that forms the blade and it's hard to imagine any way it could be made more beautifully minimal. The design is considered such a classic that it has featured on Swiss stamps – pretty good for such a prosaic item.

The Dalson 'Aussie peeler' (*centre, below*) was also designed in 1947, by the Dalsonware company in Melbourne, Australia. It has the same kind of pivoting blade as the Rex but in line with the handle in the English fashion.

What is most strange about peelers is how weirdly regionally specific they are. One would imagine that the action of vegetable peeling would be similar the world over and that the tool would have evolved to fit common practice. Instead, many different types have sprung up* and different cultures have adapted to their use.

---

* There are over 500 patents on record for various hand-held potato peelers, all clearly different from each other.

PEPPER GRINDER

SMALL MECHANICAL SPICE MILLS have been recorded in use in kitchens since the 14th century – pestles and mortars stretch back into prehistory – but spice dealers in cities made much of the grinding and preparation of spices. If you could sell the same spice ground, you had added both value and quite possibly one or two adulterants to make the expensive spice stretch further.

At the tables of the rich there had long been decorative containers for ground pepper and crystalline salt, but the grinding would have been done fresh each day by staff. After exposure to moist air both would clump up unattractively and the pepper would begin to lose its pungency.[*] It was only in the 1920s, when the various industrial salt refiners began adding anti-caking agents to table salts, that the salt shaker became not just the delivery method but also the storage container. Alongside this, pre-ground pepper, black or white, could be served in a matching container – a set sometimes referred to in the UK as a 'cruet'.[†] For many years the cruet was a relatively high-status object – there is an old theatrical joke about boarding houses charging a shilling a night for bed and breakfast and 'sixpence for use of the cruet'.

In post-rationing years, once decent-quality peppercorns were again freely available, many cookery writers began to specify 'freshly ground black pepper' in recipes. White pepper, long the dusty British grocery store staple, was nowhere near as exotic or strongly flavoured as the black peppercorns favoured by other European cuisines.

The 'burr grinder' comprises two roughly conical metal pieces, one fitting inside the other. The surface where they meet is roughened with 'burrs' – the metalworker's term for a sharp raised edge. The distance between the burred surfaces is adjustable with a simple screw, and a hand crank or knob turns one cone against the other. This mechanism cracks each corn rather than crushing or smearing it, so the pepper doesn't heat up and drive off the volatile oils.[‡]

The best example of this type is still made by the Peugeot company (*opposite, right*). They began making hand coffee mills in 1840, patenting a system of precision-cut helical burrs that drive the food down on to the cutting space. The undisputed classic design is the 'Paris' model that, according to their website, comes in all sizes from a pert 12 centimetres (5 inches) to a more boastful 30 centimetres (12 inches).

At the height of London's 'trattoria boom' in the late 1960s the tableside theatre of plying the giant grinder was so enjoyed by waiters[§] and customers alike that models up to an eye-watering metre in length were often proudly displayed.

---

[*] In a large staffed kitchen leftover pepper would be collected and used the following day.

[†] Cruet is the ecclesiastical term for a small vessel used in the Eucharist for holding water or wine.

[‡] This is the reason that coffee lovers prefer burr grinders for their beans. They run cool even when driven by a powerful electric motor.

[§] Older front-of-house staff still refer to an oversized pepper grinder as a 'Rubirosa' after the Dominican playboy and diplomat of that name … and can explain why.

WHISKS

THROUGHOUT HISTORY and all over the world, cooks have stirred with sticks, but many discovered that lighter mixtures are better beaten with a bunch of small twigs. Thin, flexible strips with space between them introduce air into the mixture and, when applied with enough vigour, can actually create stable foams and froths.

Many patterns of wire whisk have been invented over the years, perhaps the commonest being the 'balloon' type, which probably originated in professional kitchens in France. Smooth, curved and flexible, the balloon whisk fits perfectly with a deep hemispherical bowl – preferably copper – and when operated vigorously by a brawny servant will produce reliably stiff meringue, time after time.

In the domestic kitchen, though, something smaller and lighter would usually suffice. The 'gravy whisk' comprises a spring held into a loop by a thicker wire armature and mounted on a handle so as to fit beautifully on the bottom of a flat pan. Made in their millions by kitchenware companies all over the world, gravy whisks are ideal for scraping the very last atoms of goodness off the bottom of the frying pan and incorporating them into a smooth liquid sauce.[*]

So successful were gravy whisks and electric beaters in American kitchens that the balloon whisk was all but forgotten until a wonderfully eccentric woman named Julia Child made her first television appearance in 1963. Child was promoting her cookbook *Mastering the Art of French Cooking* on a TV show called *I've Been Reading …* and used the archaic and exotically 'French'-looking balloon whisk to thrash up a meringue. It was a clever visual gimmick. The broadcasters began to receive phone calls asking where these magical objects could be obtained and Child was swiftly commissioned to do the cookery shows that made her a household name.[†]

---

[*] Nobody likes to split a sauce and so, when a cook finds a whisk that works, they can become unreasonably attached to it. I still insist on using my grandmother's gravy whisk. It has never failed me in a mayonnaise or an emulsion, yet every other type has at some point disappointed me. Nobody is allowed to touch my whisk.

[†] It's one of those odd quirks of culinary history that, without the balloon whisk, Child might have remained an obscure specialist food writer rather than a global star – she certainly seemed to believe so. For the rest of her life she continued to collect whisks.

PESTLE AND MORTAR

IF WE DEFINE COOKING as the practice of changing foodstuffs to make them more palatable, then we know from archeological finds that crushing and grinding were among our first methods of doing it. Pairs of crushing stones, either selected or shaped to fit together, were used to make tough food edible before we could cut it or heat it with fire. Thus the idea behind the pestle and mortar* is culturally universal and so old as to make any notion of 'invention' pointless.

At various times in kitchen history, however, different kinds of pestle and mortar have been fashionable. The 'Wedgwood' pestle, made of unglazed porcelain and with a wooden handle, is probably the version that most immediately springs to the Western mind. It was designed in 1759 and was originally intended for use by chemists and pharmacists. The very slightly coarse surface of the porcelain is extremely tough and makes short work of reducing crystalline materials to very fine powders without tainting them in any way. The abrasive surface calls for a lateral grinding action rather than pounding. It is also easy to clean, which makes it ideal for use in the lab. In the kitchen, it's a tremendous tool for crushing sugar and salt, but does a truly miserable job of woody herbs or leafy material. In the 1930s when modernist designers took inspiration by imagining the kitchen as a 'home laboratory', the Wedgwood mortar very much looked the part in spite of its inefficiencies.

Brass mortars are best adapted to heavy vertical pounding. This makes them great for coffee beans and nuts, which need to be crushed rather than powdered.

Certain mortars have gained popularity around particular recipes. Interest in Provençal cooking in the UK in the 1970s led to a glut of decoratively painted yellow-glazed ceramic mortars with wooden pestles, which were believed to be key to a good mayonnaise. In the US at the same time the larger stone *molcajete* – essential for the very best guacamole – began appearing in kitchens. In the early 2000s, TV chef Jamie Oliver began promoting the coarse, heavy granite mortars used across India and Southeast Asia. These have a more abrasive surface than the Wedgwood type, enabling grinding, and were robust enough for vertical smashing too. Though they were a pain in the lower back to move around the kitchen, they were pretty good for everything from an Italian pesto to Lebanese *kibbeh* lamb and neatly summed up the culinary multiculturalism of the era.

At the time of writing, many cooks are discovering the Japanese *suribachi* (*left*), a light ceramic bowl with an interior roughened by dragging a comb through the wet clay. It's great at pulping tough roots as well as woody spices and is sometimes used with a *surikogi* or pestle made of fragrant wood† – unlike previous forms, the intention is for the stick to be worn down and affect the flavour of the food.

---

* In Latin, *mortarium* means 'receptacle', *pistillum* means 'beater'.

† Often the wood of the *sancho* (Japanese pepper) tree.

GARLIC PRESS

THE GARLIC PRESS may be one of the simplest items in the kitchen drawer but it's also the most socially divisive. The basic model is a two-piece alloy casting that enables the user to exert a little extra leverage on an individual garlic clove. A key benefit is that one doesn't need to peel the clove before crushing. With a garlic press one can minimise handling of the clove and prevent the smell lingering on the fingers.

The garlic press was an obvious early choice for stocking in Habitat. It was cheap, functional, a classic French design and unfamiliar to an older generation. For many, the garlic press was almost representative of the store itself – a tiny metal synecdoche – and it certainly fitted well with the aspirations of young customers, experimenting with exotic flavours.

A garlic press costs pennies and should be a convenience and labour-saving boon in any kitchen, but it definitely didn't appeal to everyone. Elizabeth David, at her most magisterial, wrote in *Tatler*:

'*I regard garlic presses as both ridiculous and pathetic, their effect being precisely the reverse of what people who buy them believe will be the case. Squeezing the juice out of garlic doesn't reduce its potency, it concentrates it, and intensifies the smell. I have often wondered how it is that people who have once used one of these diabolical instruments don't notice this and forthwith throw the thing into the dustbin.*'

The tension of clashing prejudices is palpable in her rage. It's distasteful to smell like a Marseille docker, yet there's a kind of naff, lower middle-class daintiness in avoiding it. Time-pressed professional chefs would simply crush garlic with the side of a blade. This cheap gadget, which subtly promised a degree of garlic avoidance, was a lovely, wide-open target … and an instant shibboleth.

One is not usually required, as a cook, to hold strongly partisan opinions on gadgets. The egg slicer leaves most of us unmoved, the cherry stoner is much of a muchness – but, as in the most bitterly fought politics, once an authoritative opinion is expressed, a line is drawn in the sand. It is impossible not to choose sides. Not only can whipping out a garlic press cause a sharp intake of breath in even the most non-judgemental of cooking companions, but thousands of words of blogs and columns have been written on both sides of the debate. Some cooks swear they can detect a metallic taste in garlic that's been through the crusher. Sources from gangster movies to food scientists are quoted in support of shaving, grating or mincing with salt, and the briefest of online searches will turn up dozens of side-by-side comparisons.

For a product designer, it would be hard to see the garlic press as anything but a brilliant piece of kit, but for the rest of us embroiled in the 'garlic press schism', it must remain, forever, a signifier. You and I may have a garlic press in our kitchens. I wish you well with it but, if you value your reputation, never show it to anyone else.

TORTILLA PRESS

IN EUROPE, we are used to yeasted breads and have equipped our kitchens accordingly with dough hooks on our mixers, and with loaf tins and computerised electric breadmakers, but probably half of the world's cuisines feature unleavened flatbreads, hand rolled and cooked on a flat plate or griddle.

The traditional methods of making flatbread usually involve a rolling pin and a kind of dextrous hand flipping that both flattens and stretches the dough. In areas where kitchen arrangements are centred around a fire on the ground rather than standing at tables or benches, a small rolling board is used. Across south Asia the board is called a chakla and the thin rolling pin a belan (see page 48).

Intriguingly, the same design of labour-saving device has appeared in both Mexican and Indian home kitchens in the form of a chapati or tortilla press. These are often roughly made – some of the castings seem to be locally copied from commercial versions – and comprise two plates, hinged with a bolt, and a lever to apply pressure to a ball of dough. Because chapati dough is flour-based and easy to handle, the Indian version of the press sometimes has two highly polished stainless steel plates that enable quick release of the finished bread. The Mexican version, which presses sticky nixtamalised corn, is used with two sheets of polythene to create a 'non-stick' surface.

Though the chapati/tortilla press isn't yet a fixture in every kitchen, the exciting intermingling of international food cultures means it is surely only a matter of time before everyone has a 'flatbread press'.

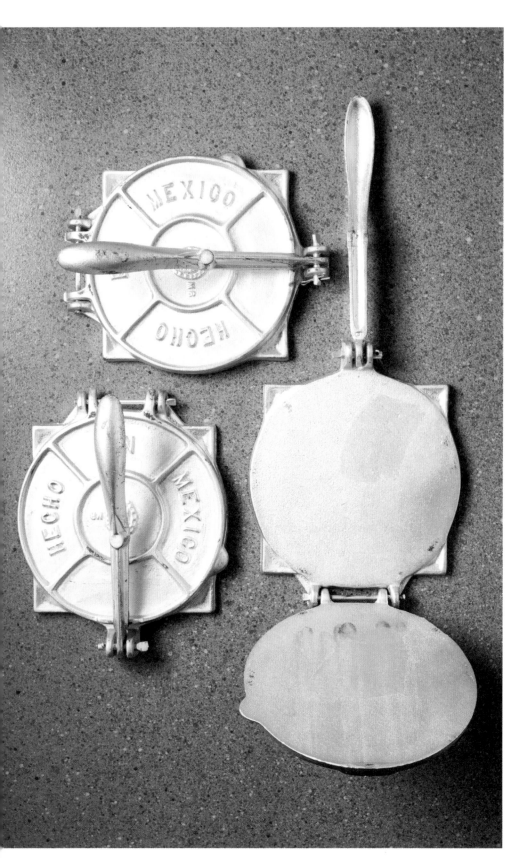

WOODEN CHOPPING BOARD

THE BEECH WOOD chopping board is an extremely functional and professional piece of equipment. Beech is a tough timber with a straight grain that is dimensionally stable when it's dry and seasoned, and cleaves easily. A chopping board is assembled of lots of regular blocks of beech that are stood on end and clamped tightly together, usually with a tensioned metal band. If a chopper or cleaver blade is swung into the board, the wood splits before the blade and is then forced back into position when the blade is withdrawn. This quality of yielding and self-healing has made beech the working choice of professional butchers for centuries.

In farmhouses or the kitchens of large stately homes, there was a need for in-house butchery. Whole carcasses would be delivered and had to be turned into neatly trimmed cutlets or smartly rolled joints, but the domestic kitchen has no need for chopper or cleaver.

A small beech chopping board became a fashionable accessory in home kitchens where a rustic aesthetic was required, but the end-grain structure meant that the board had to be several inches thick and was correspondingly heavy. The board looked lovely but was a bugger to lug to the sink for proper cleaning.*

Today, 'end-grain' block is one of the most popular finishes for fitted kitchen worktops. Long runs of the material can be machine-made from small blocks of recycled timber and retain just enough of the visual cues of the traditional kitchen to please modern cooks. Nevertheless, they protect their expensive worktops with nice, easy-to-clean polypropylene cutting boards.

---

* Butchers scrape the surface of their blocks with a purpose-built flat blade, removing a layer of blood-soaked sawdust every day. It's the cleaning process rather than the constant chopping that wears the block down, so it has to be replaced regularly ... or better still, sold second-hand to a householder, who will use it as an expensive 'shabby chic' kitchen sideboard and gleefully show off its patina to friends.

MINCER

IN A KITCHEN run by servants, 'leftovers'* were rarely a problem. For every aristocratic mouth to be fed upstairs there were several downstairs with no less need of nourishment. But once control of the kitchen returned to the householder the using up of surplus became a serious issue. The word appears in 'domestic management' handbooks at the turn of the century, comes into more common use during the Second World War and surges in the 1950s. An older generation can remember a time when the 'Sunday joint' was reheated in its gravy on Monday, served as sandwiches on Tuesday and, if it survived long enough, was minced for pie filling or rissoles.

The meat grinder or mincer was invented[†] in Germany in the early 1800s and it immediately made life easier for butchers, farmers, charcutiers and anyone who had hitherto been mincing fresh meat with knives. The Porkert company of Skuhrov nad Bělou in the Czech Republic have been making hand-cranked mincers[‡] since 1881. These massively cast pieces range in size from something that can be discreetly clamped to a dining table to bulky units that look like they need a couple of strapping farm labourers to turn them. These mincers were intended to deal with fresh meat, but cooks soon realised they could be used to reduce other ingredients to paste. There were even health and diet gurus who championed mincing as a way of making food 'more digestible'; the spiralizer craze of recent years proves that there's nothing new about subverting technology in pursuit of absurd diet claims.

While the great Porkerts have a design that appealed to the professional butcher, smaller mincers were marketed by appealing to notions of delicacy of preparation and thrift. The domestic mincer pictured opposite, made by Spong of Basildon, is highly stylised to appear modern and efficient. The colour might seem a little sudden to us today but, in comparison to the raw cast metal of its predecessors, it gave a clear signal that this was a refined piece of home kit. It could never reduce a pig to paste, but could elegantly turn out fashionable 'Salisbury steaks' or 'veal cromesquis' without risk to the cook's manicure.

The Spong was probably the last gasp of the hand mincer, being quickly replaced by the even more refined 'Jeannette' from Moulinex, a mincer and early food processor in candy colours. This also shredded vegetables and removed any danger of unseemly perspiring by having a powerful electric motor.

---

* There is no need for the word 'leftover' in a world where all food is naturally used up. The idea that a single meal should be seen as a discrete event rather than part of the continual feeding of the household is very much the product of modern marketing.

† By Karl Friedrich Christian Ludwig, Baron Drais von Sauerbronn, a prolific innovator and devout revolutionary. He was also responsible for the hand-cranked railway car (Draisine) beloved of Wile E. Coyote and the foot-propelled, pedalless wooden bicycle (Laufmaschine) that has recently seen a resurgence of popularity amongst the infants of the well-heeled.

‡ The company also casts the metal frames for concert pianos, a fact for which I am indebted to Twitter and Mr Jiří Schneider of Prague.

MEAT MALLET

THE STEAK, A LARGE JUICY tranche of premium meat, is a high-status dish in any culture and as such, in the natural scheme of things, is subject to cunning practice and trickery. For most, the key quality of a good steak is tenderness – pieces from lesser animals or from other than premium cuts are usually hard to chew – and so 'tenderising' has long been an important technique in commercial butchery.

Meat can be beaten out flat with a rolling pin or a flat 'meat bat', but it will tend to contract again on hitting the hot pan. The tenderising mallet forces broad points between the fibres of the meat, loosening the structure.

Used carefully and on the right piece of meat, tenderising works well. Cheaper cuts of meat such as rump cap or top round often have more flavour, so successful tenderising has given rise to a whole slew of delicious recipes, many of them designed in such a way as to conceal the trauma on the meat's surface – chicken-fried or 'cube steak' in America, 'cutlets', Swiss or smothered steak in other countries, and in every French brasserie as the ubiquitous 'minute' steak.

Commercial tenderising is done with heavy mallets or even comb-like structures of blades that actually pierce the meat along the grain, but the domestic steak mallet is always just a little too light to do a great job. It's also true that a butcher will always be happy to tenderise steak for you professionally before it leaves the shop – which leaves one wondering whether the mallet we all remember in every kitchen we've ever been in isn't actually the single most inadequate and pointless kitchen tool ever made.

Perhaps the clue is in the status of the steak. In the past it was a rare treat in most domestic kitchens, and many would never have seen one from one end of the year to the next. In these homes though, is there not perhaps a case for the tenderiser as a symbolic object? A man might, in the past, have hung a spear or a favourite hunting rifle on the wall to remind guests that he could hunt and provide meat for his tribe. The meat mallet, hanging on the rack, on show, tells guests that, yes, this is the kind of house where we can afford steak.

'MOULI' GRINDER

THE FOOD MILL – often colloquially referred to as a 'Mouli' – domesticates and simplifies one of the most labour-intensive jobs in the professional kitchen.

The traditional way to reduce food to a smooth purée was to pass it through a sieve. This meant forcing ingredients that are either naturally soft or have been cooked to softness through the tight mesh. In a kitchen with servants or lower-grade chefs, this had never been a problem. There are references to kitchen slaves in ancient Rome having been assigned the miserable, exhausting task. Eventually someone (it would be nice to think it was a commis with extremely sore arms) came up with the idea of a rotary scraper set inside a sieve, and what was arguably the first 'food processor' was born.

There had been many forms of this simple device, but the classic is the 'Moulinette' vegetable mill introduced at the Lyon Fair in 1932 by its designer Jean Mantelet. Priced at a steep 36 francs, the gadget had few takers, so two months later, at the Paris Fair, he reduced it to 20 francs – probably a fairer price considering that it was mass-produced from the simplest of pressings. By the end of the year he was producing 2000 per day.

Mantelet went on to invent a range of cheap kitchen gadgets, including the Mouli-Noix nutcracker, the Mouli-Râpe vegetable scraper and the Mouli-Sel, a salt grinder. Never one to let a good idea go to waste, in 1957 he finally changed the name of his company from the unwieldy mouthful Société d'Etudes Chimie et Méchanique to the snappier Moulinex.

The design has changed little from the original, with the crank handle driving a spiral pusher that mashes the food through a plate pierced with holes. The plates are interchangeable, enabling a degree of control over the coarseness of the purée produced and also, much like the kitchen mincer, allowing tough materials to be fed several times through decreasing gauges.

The Mouli is still a popular tool. Though many of its functions are effortlessly performed by the Robot-Coupe (see page 72) or other electric food processors, it is easier to dismantle and clean. It also has less tendency to whip everything into an instant mush and is therefore useful when preparing baby food. As it acts by squeezing food through holes rather than cutting it with blades, it can also do less damage to the cellular structure of the food, meaning, for example, that it can make smooth mashed potato that isn't 'gluey'.

GRATER

THE BOX GRATER common in most kitchens is usually attributed to French inventor François Boullier who is supposed to have devised it in 1540 so that hard leftover cheese could be rendered edible for the poor. Though the effort was laudable in its intent, Boullier's claim can only be false. The Japanese have had their traditional graters (*oroshigane*) for much longer – though, to be fair, they are comparatively late converts to the idea of cheese. Cheese graters certainly existed in ancient Greece,* but you'd have to imagine they were actually invented long before by any civilisation with the equipment to bang a spike through a piece of sheet metal and wiggle it about. This intuitive method of punching a hole and distorting the edge to create a sharp burr is still more or less the process used to make traditional graters to this day.

Grating is one of the earliest and most efficient methods of 'food processing'. Tough material can be chopped with a knife – but that's hard work and leaves big chunks. It can be pounded in a pestle and mortar, but that destroys all texture. The grater is effectively a set of hundreds of small knives, each taking regular-sized strips out of the food. The speed and simplicity of the operation and the utter textural regularity of the finished food makes the grater a brilliantly effective tool at a low price. It's one of the kitchen tools that most obviously replicates the work of a skilled kitchen servant in the domestic setting and it's almost impossible to imagine it could be improved on …

It was in 1949 that an efficient hardened steel grater was first patented in Australia as a woodworking tool. Unlike a file it didn't clog and it was great at rapidly removing material when forming surfaces. The 'Surform' survived, with minor improvements, until 1985 when a company called Grace Manufacturing in Arkansas came up with a genuine innovation. They had been making printer parts by etching them out of stainless steel sheet with ferric chloride – a process with the inconvenient side effect of producing razor-sharp edges. Their first product utilising their accidental discovery was a woodworking tool, but by the mid-1990s they'd realised that more cooks than woodworkers were buying their 'Microplane'.

In just a couple of decades, Microplanes have taken over from graters in the kitchen. They are available in different gauges and can even be bought mounted in a chassis that apes the early box grater. The incredible precision of the etching process, though, has also improved the way that ingredients can be prepared. Hard Parmesan can be reduced to soft, airy drifts, garlic and ginger can be effectively liquefied and chocolate can be shaved into incredibly regular and aesthetically pleasing curls.

---

* *Iliad* 11.640 Hecamede uses one to grate goat's cheese over Nestor's cup of Pramnian wine. There are also tantalising references in the first scene of Aristophanes' play *Lysistrata* to a sexual position: 'The lioness on a cheese grater'. It's worth Googling.

KITCHEN KNIFE*

THE 'CHEF'S' KNIFE is a surprisingly late addition to the home kitchen. Though professionals have, for as long as anyone can remember, wielded a large knife for tasks large or small, most home cooks have justifiably found such a tool to be beyond their needs and quite possibly dangerous. In the domestic setting, cutting was often done sitting down and slicing veg towards the thumbs, with whatever small knife was closest to hand. In a way this is the most natural approach and quite sufficient for home cooks. It was only the insistence of writers like Elizabeth David and Robert Carrier in the 1950s that drove people to invest in the then state-of-the-art Sabatier kitchen knife – leading to a whole series of changes in behaviour ranging from regular sharpening to chopping while standing up.[†]

The Sabatier was a truly totemic piece of kit for the growing band of keen home cooks. It was made of carbon steel, which meant it went black when used on onions or lemons. It had to be sharpened regularly, you needed to take time to learn how to use it and you would cut yourself many times in the process. It's impossible to imagine any other piece of kitchen equipment surviving such a learning curve without being dumped for something simpler and safer, and yet such was the symbolic significance of the knife that home cooks persisted.[‡]

Today, buying one's first expensive kitchen knife is pretty much the defining action by which food lovers declare themselves – by bringing a professional tool into a home setting. Investing in a decent knife is felt to be the moment at which one ceases merely to cook for one's family and begins to *be* 'a cook'.

---

[*] Knives are so endlessly fascinating that someone should write a book about them (Tim Hayward, *Knife: The Culture, Craft and Cult of the Cook's Knife*, Quadrille 2016).

[†] When a small knife cuts toward the thumb, it can be used sitting or standing, but a larger knife has to be used in a downward movement against a cutting board. For people of normal height, this is uncomfortable on a kitchen table – traditional standard height 760 millimetres (30 inches) – which explains why the standard height for a kitchen counter is 900 millimetres (35½ inches).

[‡] When first mentioned by British writers, Sabatiers were only available from a few catering supply specialists. In common with Le Creuset pots, Sabatiers became truly popular when Terence Conran began stocking them in Habitat.

LEMON SQUEEZER

IT'S AN OFTEN QUOTED axiom that if you 'build a better mousetrap, the world will beat a path to your door' and one would expect this to be particularly true of domestic kitchen appliances. People want devices that reduce labour, that save them time or money. You would expect there to be very little interest in, let's say, a lemon squeezer that was less efficient than existing ones.

Fresh, ripe lemons are easy to extract juice from just by slicing them in half and squeezing by hand, but a simple 'reamer' helps. This is usually a wooden device, carved to fit the inner curve of the rind, with a textured surface. A lemon half is held in one hand and the reamer applied with the other. For speed, the reamer shape might have its bottom flattened and be used, single-handed, standing on a flat surface. Hundreds of patents exist for variations on the basic reamer idea – versions with levers, refinements for removing pips and pulp, and so on. One design, though, has gained possibly the greatest acclaim while being the very worst at its job.

The 'Juicy Salif' lemon squeezer was designed by Philippe Starck for the Alessi company. If the creation myth is to be believed, it was sketched on a restaurant napkin while the designer was eating a dish of squid overlooking the Mediterranean. Priced at around £43, it is a true Veblen good.* In 1990, when the Juicy Salif was launched on an eager public, high design, particularly from Italian practitioners, was becoming widely popular. It was the time when 'designer' became an adjective to be applied to clothes, household goods and the first 'designer lemon squeezer'.

A few people attempted to *use* the Salif rather than leaving it as a sculpture signalling taste from the benchtop. They would have been disappointed. The spindly legs meant applying any pressure to the lemon was impossible without it tipping over or skittering away. If you owned a glass the right size to fit under the body of the object, it sprayed a mixture of juice, seeds, pulp and frustration into it and also over a metre-diameter spatter-zone. If not washed immediately, the shiny polished aluminium surface of the squeezer began to degrade, etched by the acidic juice.

Millions of Juicy Salifs have been sold and examples rest in most of the world's design museums. The original napkin resides in a frame at Alessi's headquarters and the world looks on in baffled wonder. Alberto Alessi, who commissioned and manufactured this eccentric piece, perhaps best sums up the mystery of its success:

> *'The explanation has to do with what semiologists call the "decorative veil". The decorative veil is the space that always exists between the function and the design of an object. There is never a complete overlap. In this case, Philippe exploded that little space.'*

---

* The law of demand in economics is that when the price of goods rises, demand drops. A Veblen good breaks the law of demand as demand rises with its price. Luxury or 'designer' objects are often Veblen goods – confirming the purchaser's taste and discretion by their high price, they are, to quote one manufacturer, 'reassuringly expensive'.

ON
THE FITTED
KITCHEN

THE 'FITTED' KITCHEN can claim to be one of the oddest items in our houses. It's simultaneously a room and a piece of furniture. It's assembled to the owners' design, but within the parameters of another designer's 'units'. Its aesthetic is chosen from a catalogue and we often pay as much for it as we would for a new car. It's a status symbol and yet its history lies in political radicalism and its evolution has involved reformers and iconoclasts.

Catharine Beecher was a prolific writer and thinker on the role of the woman in society. Born in New York in 1800, she was conventionally educated, but also took on enormous amounts of study in areas not usually permitted for women at the time. She became a passionate advocate for the education of women – though she opposed women's suffrage – and in her later years turned her attention to improving efficiency in day-to-day domestic work with her book *The American Woman's Home: Or, Principles Of Domestic Science; Being A Guide To The Formation And Maintenance Of Economical, Healthful, Beautiful, And Christian Homes*. In American cities and urban centres, wealthy families had kitchens much like the European model, but large areas of the United States still practised slavery* and in others a more 'pioneer' lifestyle meant that women worked in a way that blurred the boundaries between traditional mistress/servant roles. Beecher was writing about kitchens with servants, but in a society that, in many ways, expected more involvement from the mistress of the house than their equivalents in Europe. She dedicated the book: 'To the women of America, in whose hands rest the real destinies of the Republic'.

Her approach was to analyse the space in the kitchen and to organise everything within it. Purpose-built cupboards, some of them on wheels, provided a home for every ingredient and utensil and, perhaps most importantly, she began to question the distances walked by the cook during each process. She compared the efficiency of the ship's galley where 'every article and utensil used ...

* Catharine's sister was Harriet Beecher Stowe, abolitionist and author of *Uncle Tom's Cabin* (1852).

is so arranged that with one or two steps the cook can reach all he needs' with the standard kitchen in a large house of the period, where 'the table furniture, the cooking materials and essentials, the sink, the eating room are at such distances apart that half the time and strength is employed in walking back and forth to collect and return the articles used'. Beecher's recommendations included continuous work surfaces, separate areas for preparation and washing-up and, in a few tantalising paragraphs, the suggestion of standard sizes for cupboards and shelves, and there is an assumption throughout the book that the kitchen of the future will be servantless.

Beecher's work was prescient and far-reaching, though it's difficult today to see how her desire to relieve work pressure on women could sit comfortably with the idea of denying them the vote. Perhaps the key lies in her personal religious beliefs that 'woman's mission is self-denial' and her desire to 'elevate the honour and remuneration of domestic employment according to the principles and teachings of Jesus Christ'. Her vision was of 'handsome, strong women, rising each day to do their in-door work with cheerful alertness' and that time saved through 'labour-saving' could be spent in prayer.

Christine Frederick, an American home economist, was the first reformer to apply the principles of Taylorism – sometimes called Scientific Management – to the home. Her book *Household Engineering: Scientific Management in the Home** applied the same 'time and motion' studies then being used in factories and workshops to kitchen work. She began measuring her own movements in the kitchen and later formalised the study, turning her home into the 'Applecroft Home Experiment Station' from where she continued her research until the 1940s. Many of Frederick's suggestions still make terrific sense today – she advocated draining racks so dishes could air-dry by themselves, counter heights set according to the height of the cook and narrow shelves for storing ingredients one item deep.

* Published in 1919.

Frederick's motivations seem the most purely scientific amongst the kitchen reformers; her writing implies that efficiency is sufficient reward in itself.* Indeed, her rigorous approach meant her books were keenly sought out by architects and product designers.

Frederick influenced many in the burgeoning European Modernist movement. A growing architectural avant-garde stood ready to tear down traditional notions of the domestic space and rebuild something more rational; Frederick's drive for an industrial level of efficiency chimed well with their notions of the home as a 'machine for living'. Margarete Schütte-Lihotzky† was a young Austrian Modernist working with architect and city planner Ernst May on *Neues Frankfurt*,‡ a vast social housing project. She spent two years studying the kitchens on Pullman trains and ocean liners to more efficiently design the 'Frankfurt Kitchen'. In combining Taylorist principles directly with physical measurement Schütte-Lihotzky laid the groundwork for the science that would later be called 'ergonomics'.

Henry Ford and early exponents of 'time and motion' attempted to rethink work flow and their ideas translated well to the kitchen (the kitchen triangle). Modernist designers and architects became interested in working with idealised standard measurements for the human body so form could better follow function.

In the USSR many felt that Taylorism focused too much on the efficiency of the 'man-machine system' in the pursuit of profit and not enough on the wellbeing of the worker. In 1949 these ideas

---

* Weirdly, Frederick was also the first person to suggest that 'built-in obsolescence' was a useful driver in the American economy, thus damning us all to a life of shoddily made gadgets and constant 'updates'.

† Schütte-Lihotzky remained a committed Communist all her life and during the Second World War voluntarily returned to her home city of Vienna to help mobilise Communist resistance to the occupying Nazis. She was captured by the Gestapo and imprisoned until the end of the war.

‡ *Neues Frankfurt* was built between 1925 and 1930 and employed many young architects in what was seen as a cutting-edge socialist scheme. When the Nazi government took over the project towards its end, many of the young architects fled, a wave of cultural diaspora that spread modernism across the globe. Ernst May led a small group, including Lihotzky, by train to the USSR where they worked on several huge city building projects as The May Brigade.

gelled into the new science of ergonomics. As the kitchen is the place where most domestic work is done, it's also the place where ergonomics have had the greatest effect on environmental and product design.

The Frankfurt Kitchen was mass produced to the sort of budget that made it suitable for social housing projects. It fitted into a standard 6.5 square metre (70 square feet) 'footprint', which meant that nothing was ever more than a single pace and a stretched arm away from the cook. A sliding door separated the kitchen from the living space, the overhead work light was on a sliding wire so that it could be moved wherever it was needed and a small wheeled stool made it possible to sit down while working. There was a 'waste hole' in the worktop with a bin beneath, and the dish rack was designed, in a flash of Frederickean brilliance, to drain directly into the sink. One of the most noticeable features was a set of 'drawers' that took the form of square-sided 'jugs' from which ingredients could be directly poured. This idea is perhaps symbolic of the main fault in the Frankfurt kitchen. As Schütte-Lihotzky said '… I never cooked myself. At home in Vienna my mother cooked, in Frankfurt I went to the Wirthaus. I designed the kitchen as an architect, not as a housewife'. Though the idiosyncratic drawers were of impeccable rational design, with form rigorously following function, they were labelled, thus prescribing the ingredients the restaurant-going architect felt would be appropriate to the working-class mother in her 'ideal' kitchen. Over 10,000 of the Frankfurt Kitchens were built and installed in social housing; there is, unfortunately, no record of how many actually used the drawer marked 'Reis' to keep rice in.

It would be fair to say that Schütte-Lihotzky's designs were highly influenced by her politics, with a stated aim of increasing efficiency in the home in order to get women back into work. In her later work in the USSR, particularly the design of the city of Magnitogorsk, the integration between domestic dwellings and industrial work places was much more pronounced.

It was, of course, most efficient for workers to eat communally, with food prepared in central kitchens, and this was the case in some Communist industrial cities and farms. In the UK there were several experiments with communal kitchens. At the Meadow Way Green housing scheme in Letchworth Garden City (1914); Kensal House* (1930), a slum clearance project in West London; and the Lawn Road flats (1934), a left-leaning experimental intellectual community in Hampstead (sometimes called the Isokon Building), communal kitchens and dining rooms were part of the original plan. At the Lawn Road flats the kitchen soon became a restaurant and bohemian private members' club; the working-class residents of the Kensal House scheme quickly rejected the notion and demanded individual kitchens. Only the Letchworth experiment survived with residents living, cooking and eating communally until the 1970s.

In 1927 the Dresden Hygiene Museum organised over 1200 exhibitions all over Europe, attracting over 30 million visitors. One consistent design theme that ran through all the exhibits was the use of white, hard surfaces. They reflected light, making the kitchen a brighter place to work, and were easy to wipe clean. One designer who took this to the heart of his work was Friedemir Poggenpohl. His company† had been experimenting with rational kitchen design and in 1928 launched the Reform Kitchen, a suite of purpose-designed cupboards and fittings finished with a patented 'Ten Layer' non-porous white lacquer.

The Hygena‡ company was launched in 1925 in Liverpool when furniture maker Len Cooklin teamed up with toy manufacturer George Nunn to build single-unit 'kitchenette' cabinets to

---

* Elizabeth Denby was the Social Housing Expert and Consultant who worked with architect Maxwell Fry on the Kensal House project. Between the wars she had held a Leverhulme Research Fellowship with which she had extensively researched social housing across Europe. For inexplicable reasons her name does not appear in the documentation of the project.

† Founded in 1892.

‡ It's not recorded where the name 'Hygena' sprang from, but 'hygiene' was a major selling point in kitchen equipment (see page 175).

their own original designs. It's fair to say that they pushed innovation about as far as could possibly be imagined in a single piece of furniture. Various cabinets in their extensive range featured roller shutters, a flour hopper, an egg rack, a shopping list 'reminder', bill clips, a desk and pen tray, cutlery drawers and even fold-out ironing boards and dining tables. By 1939 they were making pre-fabricated units, inspired by systems available in Holland and Germany.

Fitted kitchens and the appliances in them are luxury goods and usually the product of light engineering. For this reason, development of the kitchen pretty much ceased during both world wars as manufacturing was turned over to munitions and other war work. Many of the companies making timber furniture in the UK and the US turned themselves to aircraft manufacture. Materials like steel and aluminium were considered far more important in the manufacture of weapons than teapots and toasters. War was, however, a period of intense research and innovation.[*] In the years following both wars, aircraft manufacturers in particular found themselves with little work. Factories that had built fighters and bombers retooled to build aluminium kitchen units and cupboards and sell 'fitted kitchens' to a war-weary generation.

With so many people returning from war, social attitudes could not remain unchanged. In 1918 Prime Minister David Lloyd-George promised 'homes fit for heroes' in his housing programme. In 1944 British modernist Jane Drew organised an exhibition in London on advancing the design of the modern home kitchen. The catalogue features pictures of soldiers, sailors, airmen and war workers returning home, with the caption, 'These are the people for whom we are building'. A decent home kitchen was seen as part of the essential modern home for all classes – and women, many of whom had been in the workplace for the first time in their lives

---

[*] The microwave oven is said to have been discovered when scientist Percy Spencer stood in front of an experimental radar device and 'cooked' a chocolate bar in his pocket.

during the war, had returned with very different attitudes to domestic work.*

Companies that had been building planes, ships, tanks and guns found themselves with surplus capacity, materials, skills and staff, and the public were led to expect, if not demand, a better life at home – creating the perfect conditions for a post-war consumer boom. The United States, in many ways financially insulated from the war, began to benefit first, and by the early fifties shiny fitted kitchens and innovative electrical appliances, sold on easily available credit, began to define a new level of luxury in the kitchen.

In the UK, however, shortage and scarcity continued in many areas for decades. In 1942 the 'Domestic Furniture (Control of Manufacture and Supply) (No. 2) Order' had been put into place, restricting the use of scarce raw materials by approving only the simplest and most economical designs and restricting sales to those who could prove need.† Utility furniture was impressive in its efficiency, fitness for purpose and clean lack of ornamentation.‡ But the order held back much aesthetic development until it was finally rescinded in 1952.

Companies such as Hygena had experience of kitchen design before they'd turned to war work and for them, the evolution of design was a matter of balancing consumer aspirations with the rules restricting materials. A different path was followed by the Constant Speed Airscrews company (later CSA Industries) based in

---

* By far the majority of British architectural design in the period immediately after the war was regeneration, funded by the state. It can be argued that the material and financial restraint inherent in social projects drove much design in the direction of modernism.

† Householders, usually only newlyweds or those who'd been bombed out of their houses, had to apply for a permit to buy Utility furniture.

‡ Utility designs were in an austere style, evolved from the British Arts & Crafts movement in which some of the key designers had their roots. The basic philosophy of Arts & Crafts involved an appreciation of beauty in utility, which chimed well with the modernist style developing contemporaneously in Europe. Many design historians draw distinct links between the forcibly 'de-ornamented Arts & Crafts' of wartime utility design and post-war British modernism.

Warwick. Originally the company manufactured propeller bosses for racing aircraft.[*] During the war production was massively increased to supply propellers for both Spitfire fighters and Mosquito bombers.[†]

With production turned over entirely to such specifically war-related work, the existence of the newly expanded company was under threat when the war ended and orders naturally dropped to zero, but in 1948 the company came roaring back with the UK's first modular fitted kitchen. The English Rose was made using exactly the steel-pressing technologies used to make the fuselage and wings of an aircraft. The units were designed in the sweeping curves of a fast plane and to the design tolerances of a crafts-man-built war-machine. The kitchens were priced high – a single unit cost roughly the same as a factory worker's weekly wage – but had the tightly engineered feel of a luxury car and could be tai-lor-made to the discerning customer's personal specification. It has even been suggested that the unique overhang of the drawers allowed room for the swing of the capacious skirts of the era when clothes-rationing finished.

It would be wrong to characterise the diaspora of creatives and intellectuals between the wars as a good thing, but companies in both Britain and the US often benefitted. After the war a Hungarian emigré and visionary designer called George Fejér joined Hygena. It was his work, influenced by his modernist background, that led the company through the decades of austerity to 1969 and the launch of Hygena QA.[‡] This was the first ever system of flat-pack, self-assembly[§] kitchens – clean, modern, efficient and above

---

[*]   By varying the angle of the propeller blades, the pilot could change the speed of his acceleration while keeping the engine speed efficiently constant. Between the wars CSA made the propellers for both the British Supermarine and the German Messerschmidt entrants for the prestigious Schneider Trophy seaplane races.

[†]   …increasing the speed of both and entirely altering the balance of power between RAF and Luftwaffe.

[‡]   QA stands for 'quick assembly'.

[§]   Print advertisements for the QA kitchen showed a schoolgirl, armed with a single screwdriver, assembling a cupboard and drawers.

all, affordable – which suddenly brought the fully fitted kitchen into the reach of most families.

By the mid-1970s the self-assembly fitted kitchen had become the national norm in the UK and prices grew lower and lower as more manufacturers entered the market. A kitchen that was as good as custom-built could be had at prices so affordable, so democratic, that even the most doctrinaire of the early reformers could only have been delighted. But now that the well-designed modern kitchen was ubiquitous, it was natural that buyers should seek out ways to distinguish themselves through their choices. Reassuringly small companies began to offer 'handmade' fitted kitchens, often in pointedly retro and rustic styles, at luxury prices.

In a strange reversal of trend, wealthy householders sought out kitchens made with craft skills that wouldn't have been out of place in a stately home a couple of hundred years ago. At the same time the kitchen became 'impermanent' – housebuyers in an increasingly febrile market would, as a matter of routine, tear out a serviceable kitchen when they moved in to replace it with a 'dream kitchen' that more precisely fitted their personal aesthetics. Christine Frederick would have been both surprised and gratified to see that the kitchen had finally achieved 'built-in obsolescence'.

CHAKLA AND BELAN

CHAPATIS, ROTI and other unleavened flatbreads are common as a staple across much of South Asia and have spread worldwide with expatriate families. Flatbreads would originally have been cooked over a domestic fire and would have been made in a space that may not have had the benefit of a bench or table for preparation purposes. Skilled cooks could shape the dough by throwing it between the hands with a slapping action, but for others the chakla was an easier option. A basic round board, it is usually raised on short legs, and the bread is rolled out using a belan or thin rolling pin.

As with the Dutch Pot (see page 136) for Jamaican emigrants, a favourite chakla and belan was one of the things a South Asian family might have taken with them on leaving their homeland, in the assumption that such implements might not be available where they planned to settle. They were often passed down from mother to daughter.

In the modern kitchen, many cooks happily roll chapatis on the ample smooth work surfaces. So though there is strictly speaking no need for the chakla, it does retain its cultural and emotional significance. In a little triumph of multiculturalism, several South Asian cooks I've spoken to have adopted tortilla presses (see page 22) for even faster and more consistent chapatis.

KITCHEN SCALES

BALANCE SCALES are such a simple principle that they probably existed long before we have historical evidence for them. The Egyptians certainly used standard weights and were able to use them in trade. When food was bought and sold by weight, balance scales would be used, or the more convenient 'steelyard', a hanging beam along which a balance weight* could be slid against a scale.

In 1760 Richard Salter invented what he called a 'pocket steelyard', a device in which objects could be hung on a spring and 'weight' read off on a scale.[†] Simpler to manufacture and easier to use than other types, Salter's 'spring balances' were perfectly accurate enough for home cooking. Recipe books required repeatable, if not ounce-accurate, measurement and a spring-type scale could be pulled out of a cupboard and used without complicated setting up or zeroing. The flexibility of the spring can vary subtly over time and with extremes of temperature, but any differences were effectively negligible in domestic use.

The legal weights by which traders are permitted to sell goods must be much more accurate and repeatable, which is why most spring-based kitchen scales are marked 'not legal for trade' and why legislation requires spring balances to be calibrated regularly and temperature compensated. Today a Customs and Excise or Trading Standards officer will still spot check the scales in a commercial establishment with a set of standard 'weights' (which are, of course, really masses).

Today, electronic scales are cheap and widely available giving accurate measurements down to a tenth of a gram. Along with digital thermometers and electronic timers, they should have rendered cooking entirely foolproof. In commercial kitchens such scientific measurement has been keenly adopted and is now ubiquitous at every level from Michelin-starred restaurants to school dinner halls. What is intriguing is how domestic cooks (with the possible exception of bakers) still continue to resist such equipment as 'too complicated'. If we ever needed proof that cooking is as much to do with romance as science, this is it.

---

* More accurately a 'mass'.

† The 'weight' of an object is defined as the force upon it exerted by gravity. This is why an object of 1 kg 'mass' can 'weigh' less on the moon than it does on earth. A spring balance (also called a Newton Meter) measures the pull of gravity against a spring and so would read 1 kg for a bag of sugar on earth and about 100 grams for the same bag on the moon. A balance scale with a 1 kg weight on it or a steelyard would show the same bag of sugar as 1 kg no matter where it was set up. As almost all kitchens are subject to Earth's gravity at a relatively constant 9.8 metres per second every second, spring scales – calibrated in grams and kilograms or pounds and ounces – will remain the most robust and simple way of 'weighing' until we colonise other worlds.

CIRCULAR BREAD BOARD

I'M BEGINNING TO THINK that the wooden breadboard is a genuine mystery. Everybody remembers them. A circular board, about 30 centimetres (12 inches) across with either a carved border or a couple of simple turned lines, it came from somewhere deep in the family past. It had always been in the kitchen and, weirdly, it had the word 'bread' carved on it.

Take a look in any junk shop or cruise eBay and you'll see dozens of them – cut to bits over time, warped with over-vigorous cleaning, stained with lord knows what or burned with hot pots. But always there is that word, echoing like a taunt: bread .... Bread ... BREAD!

This is incredibly strange. Breadboards were not made by a single individual manufacturer, so this seems to be a sort of 'folk' pattern – but why? There is no functional reason that the board needs to be distinguished from other ones. It's quite a distinct board, self-evident in its size and function, and I've never seen one engraved with MEAT or FRUIT. It's not as if the pattern evolves from the manufacturing process either. The boards, usually sycamore, are turned on a lathe. It's a simple job and putting in a couple of concentric tramlines would be plenty enough decoration to please even the fussiest cook. But to take it off the lathe and hand it over to another craftsman for detailed, involved chiselling that must take about five times as long to do as making the board itself... why? And even if one team of fanatically diligent craftsmen did something so unnecessary to distinguish their own work, what insane collective national delusion could have spread the practice across a whole country?*

The closest I can suggest is the French tradition of rustic handmade boards, carved with the blessing *'Donnez nous notre pain quotidien'* around the rim, effectively turning it into a devotional object or *memento dei.* But what of the British craftsmen? Are they too reserved for such florid Gallic religiosity? Too idle to carve more than the single, easy-to-spell syllable?

I'm used to kitchen utensils having a purpose, functional or social, used to them having evolved in the face of need or desire, but the English breadboard leaves me baffled and confused and must remain, for now, a mystery.

---

* I've never managed to find a board marked *bara* or *aran.*

SALT PIG

THE SALT PIG IS ONE of those odd kitchen items that seems to have as much emotional resonance as practical functionality. Salt is naturally refined into clean crystals and needs little looking after, aside from keeping it dry and free from dust. The best way of keeping salt in a busy kitchen would be a salt pot with a close-fitting lid or a 'cellar' with a small, controllable pouring hole. As soon as salt began being refined and packaged for home use, anti-caking agents were added. Most proprietary salts were sold on their 'free-running' or 'pouring' qualities, implying that the pouring cellar was the commonest way of storing.

Nobody is quite sure where the 'pig' came from. Salt pigs start appearing in cookbooks and magazine articles around the late 1960s. There are some tenuous similarities in shape to a snout, but the nearest etymological link is to a Scottish 'salt kit', which just meant a salt pot. The shape – an open receptacle with a 'hood' – barely protects the salt but, most importantly, enables the cook to grab a handful of salt and strew it over food with a grand theatrical gesture. It might be a bit archaic, a bit functionally rubbish … but the salt pig feels great to work with.

Some salt pigs are made of unglazed earthenware, leading to the claim that its absorptive qualities help to keep the salt dry and clump-free, but many others are made from elaborate decorated glazed ceramics and seem to work just as well. It's more likely that the pig keeps the salt free-flowing because it sits, open, next to a nice warm cooker, and it encourages you to use so much salt that it has to be refilled with fresh stuff once a week.

PASTA MACHINE

PASTA IS MADE on an industrial scale by extrusion. The dough is forced through a die, the pressure supplied by the same sort of simple screw mechanism you'd find in a printing or wine press. The US Library of Congress still holds a sketch of a pasta-extruding machine drawn by Thomas Jefferson during his tour of Italy in 1787. He later had one imported to Monticello. But this was a large piece of equipment and could never fit into a domestic setting, hence most fresh pasta shapes in Italy were simple and hand-formed – like malfatti and pici – or rolled and cut like tagliatelle or lasagne.

The pasta-rolling machine was a simple idea and so similar in design to a mangle that it's impossible to trace when the first examples came into existence. There are US patents for a modest-sized rolling machine in 1906,* but almost certainly they would have been made by local artisans in Italy much earlier. The design we still favour today began to appear in the 1930s, simultaneously and from several manufacturers.

The 'Imperia' is one of the most popular of the type and was first sold in 1932. A set of smooth rollers squeezes the dough to sheets of uniform thickness selected by the dial on the side. Repeated passes through the machine on decreasing settings also improve the texture of the dough. Mounted on the clips on the back of the machine is one of a series of cutter attachments, each offering two cutting patterns. It's a gorgeous object, robustly built with highly chromed steel pressings for the frame and both cutter and roller mechanisms machined to very fine tolerances. It's not an exaggeration to say that this unchanging design is as brilliantly executed as the engine on an Italian sports car.

The Imperia, along with the Marcato 'Atlas', had always been popular with expatriate Italian families, but in the 1980s the machines suddenly gained wider popularity in the US, UK and Australia. It's been suggested that prevailing government health advice at the time – fat is bad, carbs are good – made pasta a more regular choice for many families, but there was also an increasing interest in home cooking. Lacking a *nonna*, most non-Italian families would never have experienced 'pasta fresca' before the machines became common.

Today fresh pasta is widely available in supermarkets and the Imperia is often relegated, with some regret, to the back of the cupboard.

---

* Angelo de Vito of the Vitantonio Manufacturing Company in Ohio patented his design in 1906 (U.S. Patent 812704).

WIRE SLICER

THE 'TECHNOLOGY' BEHIND using a tensioned wire as a cutting device crops up in various forms all over the world. Cheesemongers the world over use a wire to cut pieces from a large block when selling to customers, but the two examples shown in the picture opposite are interesting as examples of what one might call 'regionality' in domestic kitchen tools. Both have evolved in ways that are very specific to their countries of origin.

The 'Osti' cheese slicer (*opposite, left*) was invented in 1963 by Nils Jagd Jensen and is something of a national icon in Denmark. The wire is fixed at the handle end and the thumbwheel at the other end is used to apply tension, keeping the wire taut as it stretches with age and use. A plastic insert at the tip locates the wire further from the shaft on one side so, depending on which side you use, there are two thicknesses of cheese slice available.

The key thing to notice here is that the Osti is not really of any use on hard cheeses like a British Cheddar or an Italian Parmesan, and would make a terrible mess of soft French cheeses. For Scandinavian cheeses, though, most of which have a smooth, rubbery consistency and are eaten as breakfast slices, or used to make open-faced sandwiches or in a *kolde bord** serving, it is ideal. It would be an unusual household in any Nordic country that didn't own an Osti, yet they are largely unknown across the rest of Europe.

If you ever find the larger metal device (*opposite, right*) in any kitchen worldwide, it will most likely be described as a 'mushroom slicer'. It is enormously useful and efficient at the repetitive and fiddly task of reducing small mushrooms to precisely equal slices, but in the UK it's never used for this. As far as the Brits are concerned it is only ever used to slice hard-boiled eggs … which it does quite poorly. In spite of this we continue – a cultural as well as a geographical island – slicing our mushrooms badly with blunt knives and calling it an 'egg slicer' in the face of persistent evidence of its inadequacy.

---

*   *Kaltdbord* in Norway, *Hlaðborð* in Iceland, *Voileipäpöytä* in Finland, *Smörgåsbord* in Sweden.

BLENDER

AT THE TURN OF THE 20th century, electric motors mainly appeared in factories and workshops powering machines like lathes and printing presses that had formerly been driven by steam. Two engineers from Racine, Wisconsin, Frederick Osius and Chester Beach, saw the future in the form of a small electric motor[*] that could run on the sort of current that was beginning to be delivered to US homes. In the years before standardisation, it was important that the motor could run on a variety of unreliable voltages and with both alternating and direct current. The Osius/Beach universal motor could do all this and could also have its speed controlled with simple rheostats rather than costly mechanical gearing. This was the ideal basis for electrically driven domestic appliances, so the inventors teamed up with marketing genius Louis Hamilton and in 1910 launched the Hamilton Beach Vibrator, an 8½-inch, mains-driven 'body massager', on to an expectant world.

In 1922 Stephen Poplawski designed the first blender[†] with whirling blades in the bottom of the goblet for use in soda fountains and the Hamilton Beach Company built to his design. Osius worked with Poplawski to improve the blender and they approached a backer, a bandleader called Fred Waring, who had an enthusiasm for novelty and inventions. By 1938 Waring was vigorously promoting the Waring blender to bars and hotels and finally to the public. The blender was an instant success. An object of desire, it was an efficient labour-saver in the new post-war kitchen and once it was discovered how efficiently it chipped ice, it became the launch pad for a whole generation of frothed, slushed and brightly coloured cocktails.

The goblet blender has remained a fixture on bar and kitchen counters and, in the days before efficient domestic juicers, spawned a healthy trend in 'smoothies'. But then a serious competitor appeared in the form of the stick or immersion blender, patented in Switzerland in 1950[‡] under the tradename 'Bamix'.[§] By putting the blades in the end of a 'wand' the blender could be taken to the saucepan and moved about to ensure that every bit of food received attention. The immersion blender is also a lot less fuss to clean than the older goblet type.

In the early part of the 21st century there was a brief trend for super-blenders marketed under various trade names. It was claimed that more efficient liquification could liberate more nutrients from vegetables and possibly cure everything up to and including death. In the grand sweep of culinary history, this may rank as a climax in consumer credulity and it is mercifully now passing into distant memory.

---

[*] Factory motors were rated, like steam engines, by 'horsepower'. A motor for domestic use could only be a 'Fractional Horsepower Motor'.

[†] Usually called a liquidiser in the UK.

[‡] By the wonderfully named Roger Perrinjaquet.

[§] The blender 'beats and mixes' – *bat et mixe* in French – hence Bamix.

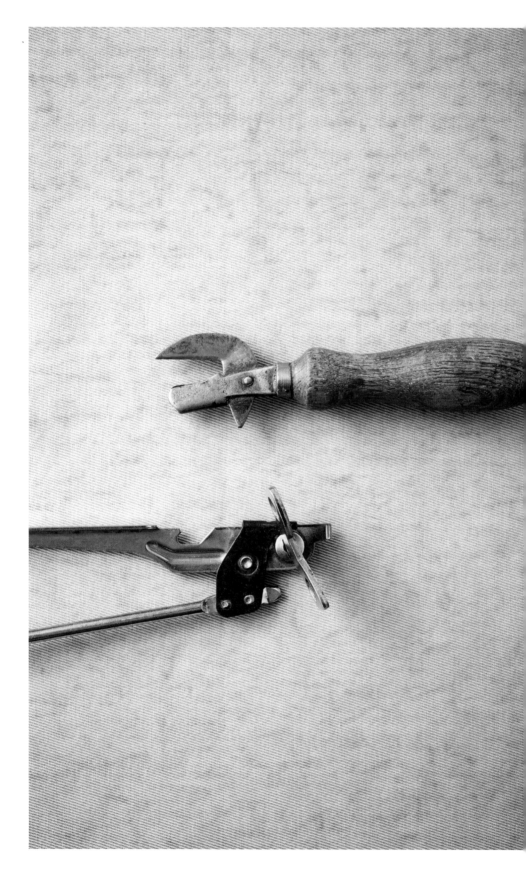

CAN OPENER

WHEN THE FIRST FOOD was canned nobody imagined there would be a domestic use for the technology. Food was preserved in bulk, usually for military or naval use, by soldering it into large wrought-iron containers in which it could be cooked. These early 'cans' would be opened with a hammer and chisel. The first patents for can openers did not appear until 1885 and these are largely variations on a chisel or thick knife.

By the mid-19ᵗʰ century, though, canned food had become a status symbol. The process was expensive, so only the best-quality food was worth using and retail prices were high. In the absence of domestic refrigeration, a tin was the best way of obtaining exotic or out-of-season ingredients with which to indulge yourself or impress guests.

Some products were only made viable at all by the advent of canning. Argentinian beef had always been salted, but shredding, cooking and hermetically packing it in tins created corned or 'bully' beef – meat with a hitherto unimaginable 'shelf life' that could be cheaply exported worldwide. Eventually the process became more efficient, prices dropped and food in cans became the storecupboard staples of the modern kitchen. It is arguable that because tinned food is of its nature already cooked and safe to eat, all one needed was a can opener and a spoon to survive. There are dire tales of bedsit dwellers today who survive on ready meals with the help of a microwave, but generations before* dined, in extremis, on tinned sardines and baked beans.

The first can openers in domestic kitchens were of the 'claw' type (*opposite, above*). A curved blade is pushed through the can lid, a pivot point is engaged on the rim and, as the cook pulls up on the lever, the opener 'walks' round the seam. With no moving parts and effectively self-maintaining, these early models lasted for generations and may still prove to be the most foolproof tool in the tough days after the forthcoming zombie apocalypse. There were, though, two main disadvantages of the claw-type opener. First, the force required to make the initial piercing of the lid, and second, the terrifyingly sharp ragged edge it left where it had effectively torn through the metal. Stabbing and sharp edges were fine for the domestic staff but needed improvement for the modern kitchen.

In 1925 the Star Can Opener Company in the US patented a design in which a hardened steel wheel cut through the can while a second wheel, toothed and geared to it, moved the cutter around the rim. The dual wheel pattern was, and remains, the ideal way to get to your dinner safely. Though the 'Star' is rarely seen outside antique shops now, the 'Bunker' opener (*opposite, below*), with its butterfly-shaped turning

---

* We may never have eaten sardines from the tin, but it's worth recalling that for much of the last century, large sections of the population would have experienced military service or living on state-supplied rations.

key and 'pliers'-style handle, is still available today, unchanged in any significant respect since it was patented in 1931.

The power to the cutting and feeding wheels could be increased with a larger hand crank and this was made easier to use by mounting the opener on the wall. Eventually, even the labour of operating a tin opener could be saved by attaching an electric motor. The first electric can openers appeared in domestic kitchens in the mid-1950s in the United States.

Our relationship with the electric can opener is complicated. It's undeniably useful but somehow smacks of 'idleness', of work avoidance, rather than labour-saving. The first electric can opener had been patented in the 1930s, but was a total flop until the very peak of post-war conspicuous consumption in the US. In the UK the electric can opener was regarded with a combination of concealed envy and open disdain. 'Imagine! Even their tin openers are electric.' And, by the time the openers were widely available and cheap, fashion had turned against canned food. The electric can opener might have been the aspirational dream, the ultimate luxury, the glittering game-show prize ... but once tinned food was regarded as downmarket, the symbol lost its status. It was truly 'a gadget too far'.

Perhaps the importance of the can opener only becomes apparent when it's lost or suddenly breaks. When you're hungry, a can of food without a can opener is an impenetrable, frustrating torture. Many cat lovers have suggested that the harmonious symbiotic relationship between our species is predicated entirely on the fact that humans alone can operate the can opener.

KITCHEN CANISTERS

SOMEWHERE BETWEEN the censuses of 1841 and 1851 the urban population of the UK exceeded the rural for the first time. A century later, in 1950, when international data began to be collated, just over 50 per cent of the populations of France, Italy and Spain became classified as city dwellers. In the UK it was closer to 80 per cent.[*] Until this point the majority of people consuming the important cuisines of Europe had been country dwellers, most with a direct relationship to the production of their food. From 1950 onwards, the majority of that population obtained all their food through other people – traders, dealers, retailers – and what was to develop into the enormous 'supply chain' of the modern food industry.

'The things we keep food in' might seem insignificant, but for me the set of kitchen canisters represents that key tipping point – what we might call 'urban majority'. Canisters are where most home cooks stored their own small stocks of dry goods. These weren't large sacks of flour that you might buy from the local mill, or the season's beans from a neighbour's field, but flour, salt and tea, purchased by the pound, wrapped in newsprint or sugar paper and brought home.

Metal canisters had always been made by itinerant tinsmiths. When diligently made, the slight flexibility of the metal and its natural tendency to spring back into shape made a seal that could keep out moisture and even be airtight. Mass production, though, made for an even better fit and so a set of canisters became essential in most home kitchens.

Unfortunately history doesn't record the genius who thought of making biscuit tins slightly rectangular,[†] but we do know that many sets of canisters were made in diminishing sizes so they could 'nest'. They were often decorated and labelled too – which must have given awesome responsibility to the designer who had to decide that the cook would need to store more flour than sugar. There's probably a thesis to be written somewhere on national, regional and class variations over history. There have been times and places where the balance has been different, and I'm not sure how many contemporary cooks would feel good about displaying vast urns marked 'Flour', 'Sugar' or 'Salt'. Modern manufacturers have been inexplicably slow to produce even larger ones marked 'quinoa' or 'chia seed'.

---

[*] Today in the UK it's about 90 per cent.

[†] The short side fits inside the longer dimension, meaning you can transport or store up to three times as many empty tins in the same space – a huge cost saving for the manufacturer.

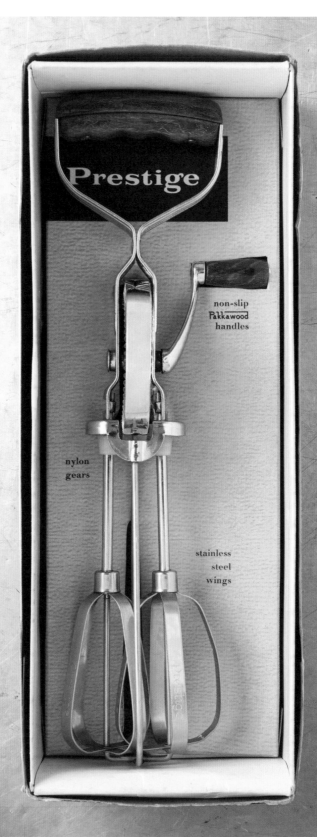

HAND MIXER

IN 1884, WILLIS JOHNSON of Cincinatti, Ohio, became one of the first African Americans to receive a patent.* He invented a mechanical egg beater that differed from the ones we might see today in that the crank drove beaters in two large tanks. The idea was that in the professional bakery one tank could be cleaned while the other was in operation. With its large capacity and range of interchangeable beaters, his machine could be said to resemble an early manual Robot-Coupe (see page 72) but the key element – a large cog driving two small ones on the beater shafts – carried on into every cranked hand blender ever since.

In professional kitchens, meringues and cream had traditionally been whipped by hard-working underchefs with huge forearms and balloon whisks, but the hand-cranked whisk, its simple gearing driving the beater heads in an impossible blur of speed, made such delicate confections possible in the home kitchen. It was a brave host who attempted a soufflé before the invention of the hand whisk, and a negligent host who didn't once it was freely available.

Whisks were an obvious candidate for electrification, but early versions were far too heavy to be hand held and uncontrollable speeds would have shot ingredients out of any but the deepest of bowls. It was not until 1964, when lighter and more controllable electric motors came on to the market, that the first hand-held mixer was patented in France.

---

* Thomas L. Jennings was the very first, granted a patent in 1821 for a dry-cleaning process.

KITCHENAID

THE ORIGINAL STAND mixer was invented by Herbert Johnson of the Hobart Manufacturing Company as a tool for commercial bakers. The back-breaking task of kneading bread dough in industrial quantities was ripe for mechanisation, so Johnson's invention took off quickly with commercial bakers and, during the First World War, was adopted as standard kit in the galleys of US Navy battleships. The story of the domestic-sized version – the KitchenAid mixer – might be one of simple slow evolution were it not for the influence of Egmont Arens.

Arens wasn't a baker or even an engineer. He began his career running a bookshop,* from which he launched a fine art press and by 1922 he had become the art editor of *Vanity Fair* magazine. His career from this point on is very much representative of the speedy evolution of American design. Through the 1920s and '30s he worked in and founded studios that answered the needs of a surging consumer economy for the first time, designing domestic goods with aesthetic as much as purely functional considerations.† The title of the book he co-authored in 1932, *Consumer Engineering: A New Technique for Prosperity*, sums up what he believed was the potential of his approach.

His company designed everything from prams to aircraft, from beer cans to jukeboxes. What was perhaps most shockingly innovative about this approach was that Arens believed that design could not only be a powerful selling tool, but also that similar design elements or themes could be equally effective across different products. In this way Arens superimposed everywhere the ideas of finned and chromed streamlining and modernity that we recall today as the 'look' of the post-war American Dream. In 1937 he was commissioned to improve the Hobart home mixer, and the 'Model K' that Arens created became a true icon of domestic design.

The KitchenAid was, of course, well engineered and efficient at its job. While other household items of the period wore out and were replaced by more modern designs, millions of KitchenAids all over the world kept rumbling on, loved and relied upon by generations of mothers and grandmothers. The company launched several updated models but none sold as successfully as the original pattern. The KitchenAid, in fact, joined that tiny group of highly characteristic, designed objects that have survived long enough into their own revival as 'retro' – perhaps the very definition of a 'design classic'. The Model K also marks the point at which a kitchen appliance was first sold and purchased as much on its symbolism as its utility.

---

* The Washington Square Bookshop, haunt of Bohemians, poets and hipsters.

† He was also, for a while, publisher of *The Playboy* magazine (a small periodical devoted to modern art) and publicly advocated for the US publication of the banned work of D.H. Lawrence and Ernest Hemingway.

ROBOT-COUPE

THOUGH THERE HAD been other devices, both electrically and manually operated, that sliced, minced or liquidised, it was Pierre Verdon, a kitchen equipment salesman, who patented the first 'food processor' in 1960 in France. The Robot-Coupe was a vertically mounted induction motor that spun blades in the bottom of a drum-shaped bowl. It used a similar principle to the blender/liquidiser, but had a 'pulse' capability for coarse chopping, and interchangeable cutting 'discs' for slicing and shredding.

The Robot-Coupe was – and remains – a phenomenally useful piece of equipment in the commercial kitchen, where its ability to prep veg to regular sizes, utterly accurately and without tiring, is a genuine blessing. In 1971 Verdon introduced it to the domestic kitchen in the form of 'Le Magi-Mix' and in 1973 it was sold to the US under the Cuisinart brand.

Though some home users find the food processor helpful, it is generally an example of a failed transition from commercial to domestic use. The processors were sold in expensive 'kits' containing dozens of accessories, promising to achieve hundreds of specialised kitchen tasks. However, the makers failed to acknowledge that in almost any circumstances, using the machine for a single process in small kitchen quantities would involve more time spent cleaning the equipment than it would take to do the job manually. The high-powered motor also made the processor very heavy, so if it didn't take up permanent space on your kitchen bench it was often too much work to get it out of storage for a small task. The food processor could do a thousand different things, but was woefully overspecced for any single one of them.*

Today food processors tend to sit idle in most kitchens, living proof that labour-saving devices don't always save labour.

---

* There is one thing that the Cuisinart can, unexpectedly, do better than anything else. In the bottom of the 'pusher' is a small hole. If you put a whole egg into the bowl and fill the pusher with oil, it will drip through at exactly the correct rate to make a completely foolproof mayonnaise.

ON
THE ROMANTIC
KITCHEN

'IN THOSE DAYS THE STREET was still a bit of a mixture. Its large, semi-detached villas had originally been built to house the Victorian middle class, then it had gone down in the world, and, though it had never entirely decayed, many of the villas degenerated into rooming houses and so were amongst the earliest candidates for what is now called "gentrification" but was then called "knocking through". Young professional couples, many of them in journalism or television, bought up the houses, converted them and (an invariable feature of such conversions) knocked the basement rooms together to form a large kitchen/dining room.'[*]

For generations the middle classes had defined themselves by the employment of servants, and houses were designed with this in mind. The kitchen was a workplace for the servants and was clearly separated. In grand houses this separation was achieved with stairs. At basement level, near the water supply and the drains, the staff could operate seamlessly: they took in deliveries invisibly through side doors, and disposed of waste at night without the family above being aware of any of the mess or work. Gorgeous food was spirited upstairs and presented as if it had materialised from nowhere.

Different design was necessary in smaller houses. Sometimes the kitchen could be separated by a butler's pantry – a tiny room, often only a couple of square metres, that functioned as a passage between kitchen and dining room. It crucially retained the possibility, or perhaps the pretence, of service staff preparing food out of sight.

Even smaller houses had to make do with a heavy door on swing hinges, so a single servant – known as a maid-of-all-work – could push through it, with hands full, to serve. This door was often covered in a thick layer of green baize which, though intended to dampen the noise of the kitchen, was also a potent symbol, a vestigial boundary between servant and served. As servants became less common and middle-class householders began cooking for

[*]   Alan Bennett, 'The Lady in the Van'. *London Review of Books* 1989.

themselves, confusion over class signifiers clung on. Keeping a separate dining room still meant you were quite well off, but simple expedients like a 'serving hatch' were social booby traps. Convenient, yes … but functioning as a kind of framed image of your reduced circumstances? Perhaps not such a good idea.

But by the mid-1960s a new kind of kitchen was becoming fashionable – one that seemed simultaneously to subvert all the firmly held rules of the previous generation and yet also turned away from many of the advances that Modernism and good design offered.

In his 1966 book *Cooking People*, Michael Bateman describes Elizabeth David's knocked-through basement kitchen in Halsey Street like this: 'Nothing gets into the house that isn't individually cared for: lovely pots from Provence, every sort of earthenware jug and pot, kitchen fittings in pine. Three dressers of unvarnished pine, two pine-wood cupboards with sliding doors, wooden plate racks, a pine table, six feet long, specially made for her.' David was symbolic of a new generation of 'knockers-through'.

The 'dresser' was a totemic object in this new style of kitchen. With drawers and cupboards below and open shelves above, dressers functioned as a service sideboard as well as a place to display crockery. In Britain, these objects, usually found in junk shops, were referred to as 'Welsh' dressers though, during their resurgence into fashion, they were sometimes rebranded as 'French' or, even more desirable, 'Provençal'. When demand for old dressers outstripped supply, new ones were manufactured and artfully distressed.

The 'scrubbed' pine table was perhaps the most significant single item in the room. Knockers-through wanted to eat in the kitchen and the table made this possible. Importantly, the table was large – the same size as the dark, polished wood, leaf-extension table that would originally have been in the dining room – but this table had the rustic finish of a farmhouse kitchen. Before mains and taps, water had been a rarer commodity in working kitchens, so the table top was often scrubbed, like a ship's deck, with an abrasive-like clean sand, or 'holystone', a naturally occurring soft rock.

Unlike the modern kitchen counter, its height set, like a laboratory or factory bench for standing work (900 millimetres), the multi-purpose kitchen table had a traditional height of 30 inches, meaning that the cook would sit down for prep work. It's difficult today to imagine how radical a change this was in kitchen use. Anyone from a middle-class background would have grown up with the importance of separation from servants drummed into them and yet now, the aspiration was towards a kitchen designed to resemble traditional servants' quarters, in which the family would gather informally. This was a place where the kids could do their homework while mother sat and shelled peas, where friends would be invited to sit, chatting freely, while the hostess threw together a simple 'kitchen supper'.

The AGA cooker was the defining object in the knocked-through kitchen. It was designed by Gustaf Dalén, a Swedish physicist and industrialist who had won a Nobel prize for his work on gas regulators in lighthouses. He was blinded in an explosion and, while recovering at home, designed the appliance when he realised his wife was becoming exhausted by the constant work of fuelling and maintaining a cooking range.

The AGA cooker was patented in 1922, and Dalén's design breakthrough was to build most of the range out of heavy iron castings rather than lighter sheet materials. Instead of a direct heat source inside the body of the oven, the AGA cooked from the radiant heat stored in the cast-iron mass. The cooker could build up heat from a constant, low-burning source and then deliver it controllably on demand. Any 'waste' heat contributed to the warmth of the kitchen.

The AGA was imported to the UK in 1929 and was an instant success. There were other range cookers and heating appliances available, but none as smartly designed and as efficient as the AGA. They were expensive, effectively luxury, items and it's sometimes assumed that they fitted naturally into large and aristocratic homes. In fact, the company made deliberate efforts to sell the cooker to the cream of society, listing in their sales material the names of owners: 'HRH Princess Beatrice, HRH Princess Alice, the Earl of Buckinghamshire, the Duchess of Hamilton, General Sir Archibald Montgomery-Massingberd, Admiral of the Fleet Sir Roger Keyes, and the Earl Nelson'. A one-time Scottish sales rep for AGA named David Ogilvy wrote what is often regarded as the urtext on high-pressure selling: 'The Theory and Practice of Selling an AGA Cooker'. He later went on to enjoy some success in the advertising industry.

By the 1930s some of the cast-iron parts of the AGA were being made at the Coalbrookdale Foundry and by 1957 all manufacture was in the UK. Sales in Sweden naturally fell away over time but in the UK sales rocketed. There were design improvements in the AGA over the years, but its unique appeal in the UK seems to have relied on its not changing much. It was worth the knockers-through spending three or four times what they'd have spent on a modern cooker in order to join a waiting list and having their floor strengthened to support such a powerfully totemic appliance.

Architecture critic Owen Hatherley pointed out in a 2013 article[*] the irony that some of the most avid knockers-through were the architects who at the time were designing social housing – the very people most versed in practical modernism and most aware of the work of people like Drew and Schütte-Lihotzky. As Alan Bennett points out, others were TV people and journalists – trendsetters and opinion formers. It is incredibly odd that at a point when the world was exploding with pop art, cutting-edge industrial design and all the cultural iconoclasm of the 1960s, Britain's creative vanguard were retiring into a kind of dreamy cosiness in the kitchen, a nostalgia for an imagined past. Unfinished low tables, dust-trap dressers and heavy iron ranges were all a wilful rejection of progress, or Escoffier's oft-quoted axiom *faites simple* taken to an almost religious level of zealotry.

[*] http://www.building.co.uk/knocking-through-the-social-divides/5050349. article

ON
THE KITCHEN
IN THE MEDIA

B Y THE EARLY SEVENTIES Vincent Price's film acting career had hit something of a slump. The horror genre that had been his main calling was in decline and he had become a regular on chat shows in both the US and the UK. He continued to work unbelievably hard, providing voiceovers for advertisements and appearing as a regular on quiz show *Hollywood Squares*. In 1971 he was approached by a UK production company to shoot six cookery shows with the working title *Cooking Price-Wise*.

The shows now exist only on a couple of VHS tapes in the bowels of the British Film Institute and do not appear on most of the lists of Price's work available online. They were certainly not high-budget productions. The clapperboard reveals they were shot back-to-back over three days, a single camera was used and there are only two names in the credits: the director/producer and company who provided the domestic flatpack kitchen units that form the set.

What's most noticeable to us today is the way that the set was so emphatically 'ordinary'. It seemed important to the pro-gramme-makers that the viewers should see the successful and wealthy Hollywood star cooking on the same chipboard-and-laminate units that they had at home. Perhaps when food on TV was still seen as instructional public information there was no need for anything else.

From the 1980s onwards there was a sense that something more than the ordinary was needed for a new food-aware audience. There began, at this point, a sort of kitchen arms race amongst celebrity chefs. Open-plan loft kitchens, warehouse apartments with spiral staircases, boutique townhouse kitchens – all pristine and aspirational – became the norm.

It would be impossible to look at the modern kitchen without recognising its place in film, TV and advertising. There are many ways that the modern kitchen is an entirely rational result of the evolution of cooking and housework but that's only half the story. Our complex relationship with this one space as a statement of status or personal worth is entirely a result of the image reflected in mass media.

The first advertising of kitchen cabinetry, appliances and tools was through catalogues – much in the same way that one might have sold farm equipment. The master or mistress of the house would look through the catalogue, perhaps at the request of the cook, and select the sort of knife polisher or cream churner that they felt would make their kitchen more efficient, but there was no attempt to ascribe any virtues beyond value for money and efficiency of use.

Things changed once the householder began choosing equipment they might have to use themselves. Advertisers had to tread a thin line between explaining how easy their equipment would be to operate, and avoiding insulting the purchaser by acknowledging that they didn't, in fact, have kitchen staff. Often they bypassed the entire question by focusing on the social cachet of a brand. AGA ovens were very successfully launched into the English market between the wars by supplying free ovens to the homes of notable public figures in exchange for discreetly listing their names in adverts (see page 77).

(see page 77)

As post-war austerity faded in the memory there was a perfect storm in kitchen advertising. There had been a general trend to encourage women back into the home so that jobs would be made available for men returning from war. As economies recovered, personal spending was encouraged with easy credit and manufacturers were able to advertise wider ranges of brighter, more modern and better-produced goods.

The 1950s and 1960s saw some of the most spectacular, if least politically sound, kitchen advertising. Impossibly beautiful female fashion models posed with fridges, cookers, rubber gloves and mop buckets. Today the use of a glamorous model to demonstrate a kitchen waste disposal would be so incongruous as to be amusing but at the time, a more acquisitive and less visually literate audience lapped up the message: 'Beautiful, rich people buy these products – you should too'.

Advertising wasn't just about kitchens, it was often set in them. As advertising became more sophisticated, setting an ad in the kitchen became a kind of semiotic shorthand, a quick and sure way to identify with the housewife viewing at home. It is remarkable, even today, how common this trope is – an ad in which two people talk about pet insurance against a blank background communicates facts like price, service and availability. Sit the same two people in the kitchen with steaming mugs of tea and the same conversation becomes a confidential recommendation between trusted friends – people just like us – that we're privileged to overhear.[*]

In 1954, art critic David Sylvester wrote a piece summing up the zeitgeist of the British art scene. He called the piece 'The Kitchen Sink', a title he'd lifted from an expressionist painting by John Bratby. Sylvester's piece describes a particularly English kind of social realism depicting not the heroism of the working class or any nobility of struggle but instead focusing on the bleakness of banal domesticity. This had less in common with Soviet art than with the contemporary philosophy of the French Existentialists.

The term 'Kitchen Sink' soon spread to other art forms, being used, pejoratively at first, to describe the films and plays of the Angry Young Men and other works of the British New Wave.

This is one of the reasons that the kitchen has played such an important role in situation comedy. It's a humanising, familiar background that immediately creates sympathy in the viewer. It's also the best room from the set designer's point of view. Most rooms in the house are focused inwards – think about those wooden Terence Rattigan dramas in rep theatres. The kind that the critic Kenneth Tynan once described as being 'set in Loamshire'. In a drawing room the seats face each other. The backdrop is wallpaper and pictures. The sofas face the audience who are effectively sitting where the fireplace might be. Performers enter and exit awkwardly from behind the protagonists.

If you talk to someone in a real kitchen you are used to their turning their back to the counter to face you. In a stage set the

* One of my favourite 'alternative' comedy shows, *The Young Ones*, was a careful and fond parody of more mainstream sitcoms. The set, naturally, was a cheap fitted kitchen that collapsed or was destroyed frequently throughout the series, or burst open to reveal members of the cast, a hamster or an atom bomb.

kitchen becomes the backdrop and the only thing between you and the performer is the dining table … at which you effectively have a seat.* We feel immediately that the play isn't just 'for us' but somehow 'about us' – because of the everyday banality of the setting.

Everything from *The Partridge Family* to *Friends* is half-shot against kitchen units so perhaps it's no wonder that we even begin to view our own family relationships against that background. In truth, it would be impossible to be exposed to mass media and not have gained the impression that the kitchen is the crucible of family life, which is probably why the design of the home kitchen has become so entangled in it.

Today, most of us aspire to 'open' 'family' kitchens. A place where mum or dad can cook while the children busily get on with improving tasks or share happy family meals. This image, fed by sitcoms and adverts for stock cubes as much as real experience, is a driving factor in the design decisions we make. In reality, we still, as we always have, eat different things at different times and kids will hide in their rooms if they can or behind their personal screens if they can't, but we still design in hope – with a great hospitable table, a groaningly packed double-door fridge and basket for the Labrador by the cooker – that the kitchen will bring us together. It's perhaps the biggest thing we've demanded from our kitchens yet – if we get the kitchen right then, like the families on the TV, we'll come together around a big old casserole and happily rub along.

---

* In 2015 the then Labour Party leader Ed Milliband chose to be photographed in his kitchen, as many politicians have, presumably in order to communicate authenticity and perhaps a kind of democratic ordinariness. It backfired horribly when the tabloid newspapers revealed that this was his 'second' kitchen, simultaneously making him seem remote from ordinary voters and duplicitous. Commentators referred to this as 'Kitchengate' and it may be the only time that a kitchen has affected the politics of a nation.

COOKING

NON-STICK FRYING PAN

IT'S AN OFT-QUOTED factoid that the non-stick frying pan was one of the spin-off benefits of the space race. In fact PTFE* was discovered by accident in 1938 by Dr Roy Plunkett at the research labs of the Du Pont Company. The polymer he discovered was unaffected by temperatures between -240°C (-400°F) and 260°C (500°F) and remained remarkably slippery. DuPont marketed the product as Teflon and it was first used in self-lubricating components.[†]

The problem with such a slippery, non-adhesive product was getting it to stick to anything, and it wasn't until 1961 that a French engineer, Louis Hartmann, cracked the problem. By etching a metal with acid, spraying it with Teflon emulsion and then baking it at 400°C (750°F) he was able to get the material to flow and create a film of TEF-lon firmly bonded to AL-uminium, giving him the catchy trade name of TEFAL.

For decades Teflon 'non-stick' pans were a hit in home kitchens. Domestic cookers were comparatively low-powered and the heat they gave out was patchily distributed. Aluminium spread the heat more efficiently than other metals and the Teflon coating usually stayed well below 260°C (500°F) – the top of its performance envelope. Better-quality stoves that could put out higher temperatures caused the coating to degrade and flake off, particularly if metal utensils were used in the pan.

Teflon pans are still made and are very popular, but new non-stick materials, including ceramics, are applied to more premium pans that might be required to run hot on more efficient modern stoves.[‡]

Teflon did eventually go into space. It was one of the few plastics that could stand the extremes of temperature. In fact, rather than the non-stick pan being a spin-off of the space race, it would be more accurate to say that PTFE was actually one of the materials that made space travel possible.

---

* Polytetrafluoroethylene.

† Its resistance to corrosive materials at high temperatures meant that the first uses of PTFE were as joint components in the Manhattan Project (1942–6), leading to the creation of the world's first atomic bomb.

‡ As professional chefs are aware, uncoated pans like cast iron skillets are effectively 'non-stick' at sufficiently high temperatures, but these temperatures would quickly degrade Teflon.

COPPER SAUCEPAN

THE FIRST METAL COOKWARE was almost certainly copper. It's easy to cast, easy to beat out and, though it's too soft by itself for edged tools or weapons, it makes an excellent pot. Through the ages we've made pots and pans out of many other metals, but copper remains the best. It transmits heat more efficiently than any other metal and the heat will spread faster, farther and more evenly through copper.

Unfortunately copper also corrodes in the presence of acid foods, producing a mildly toxic oxide, and it's easy to scratch. For this reason, copper pans in later years have been lined with other metals – often tin, which is simple to apply and effectively non-stick with careful use.

The professional kitchens of stately homes and restaurants were equipped with vast 'batteries' of copper pots, ranging from tiny sauce pots, no bigger than a teacup, to vast rectangular turbot pans a metre across, or stockpots so large they were impossible to move once filled, and had to be equipped with a tap at the bottom to draw off the liquid. The ranks of gleaming copper had to be polished daily by squads of servants, and so it was not surprising that copper became a must-have in the aspirational home.

Copper being an expensive metal, cheaper alternatives to pure copper pans have evolved. Copper can be plated over the outside surface of a stainless steel pan, which looks good aesthetically, but performs poorly.[*] Compound pans have also been made with copper bottoms for performance and a body of a more economical metal. Any popularity these strange hybrids have enjoyed can probably be blamed on a quirk of English usage. In the 18th century the British navy pioneered the use of copper sheathing to prevent the hulls of wooden warships being attacked by 'shipworm'.[†] The term 'copper-bottomed' passed into common usage to describe a firm guarantee. It was the natural association with this term that made 'copper-bottomed' seem a benefit in a saucepan rather than a cost-driven compromise.

Although they don't work on modern induction cookers, copper saucepans are still a delight to cook with. The incredible conductivity, which spreads heat so quickly and evenly through the pan, means that it can dissipate almost as quickly. The first thing the modern cook will notice is the same increase in 'controllability' that impressed Escoffier.

---

[*] Stainless steel has about a twentieth of the thermal conductivity of copper.

[†] *Teredo navalis.*

GARLIC POT

THE GARLIC POT doesn't really exist in any culture that's at ease with the use of garlic. In France, Spain or Italy, it might be hung in 'grappes', in India or China it might be kept in a pot or box, but in the UK our relationship with the stinking bulb is more complex.

Garlic is easy to grow, simple to store and usually fairly cheap to obtain. Throughout culinary history, this has meant that the poor have been able to use it as a flavouring. If your main source of nourishment is cheap starch – pasta, potatoes, rice, grits or bread – then a little garlic can spread its flavour a long way.[*] Smelling of garlic, therefore, was often seen as an indicator of poverty.

Most countries maintained a healthy interchange between the foodways of the gentry and the peasantry, but in England refinement in taste prescribed rigid separation. Early English recipe books, most notably Mrs Beeton's, were profoundly scathing about garlic and over time the country developed an almost pathological national distaste for it.

It was only with the liberalisation of international travel after the Second World War that the English discovered what they had been missing. The less well-off returned from package holidays still complaining about 'oily' food 'stinking' of garlic, but the cosmopolitan middle class embraced it keenly.[†]

Garlic was still bought by-the-bulb at British greengrocers and at a fairly luxury price point. There are many excellent post-rationalisations for the garlic pot – that its ventilation holes allow the bulb to stay dry, that the earthenware takes on the flavour or even that, through some complex light trick, the cloves are prevented from sprouting, but all these myths miss the real point. A garlic pot exists solely so that having been unable to afford a showy string of the stuff, you can proudly display your bulb in a clearly labelled pot. Like a holy relic in a monstrance it's a public pronouncement of belief: 'This is a modern, middle-class kitchen. We proudly use garlic.'

---

[*] According to Henry Mayhew, social reformer and author of *London Labour and the London Poor* (1851), the English poor often made do with cheap bread and raw onion for similar reasons.

[†] Garlic pots were popular souvenirs for many who'd had their culinary horizons expanded on holiday.

WOK

IT IS ENTIRELY UNFAIR to think of a wok as just a Chinese frying pan. It is probably the single most versatile piece of all kitchen equipment and existed in other countries before popping up in China.* Imagine the wok less as a pan than as a brilliantly shaped cooking surface. Placed over a fire, the centre of the wok becomes very hot very quickly, using the smallest possible amount of fuel. Food is dropped into the hot spot and then moved around the curved surface – tossed as gravity drags the ingredients back to the centre. Compared with flatter-bottomed Western pans, the wok puts food in contact with a higher heat, in short bursts, many times. A wok cooks food crisper on the outside and more evenly. The thin metal walls take on, transmit and lose heat quickly so, though the heat of the fire may be difficult to control, the amount reaching the food can be precisely managed by lifting the wok on and off the heat source.

The wok can also be used to boil, steam, deep fry, braise and stew. Given its versatility as an appliance for translating and directing heat for cooking, it's probably fair to think of the wok in the same way as we think of our own stoves.

This combination of wok and fire has followed an entirely different evolutionary path from the oven/stove/pot/pan model we are used to in the West. Until comparatively recently, most wok cooking for ordinary families would have taken place outdoors or in a covered area partially open to the elements. Temperatures much higher than anything achievable on a Western domestic stove were standard. In fact, it is only in recent years, as the wok has become popular with Western cooks, that burners of anything like the power required have been available domestically here.

A proper wok will work on a large (usually 5 kilowatt) gas burner, though it often requires a special ring to hold it over the flame. Flat-bottomed woks – the only ones that work on electric or induction hotplates – mean that the food tends to stay still in the bottom, giving stewed rather than crisp results.

Modern woks for home use are made of steel or cast iron and, though many Western chefs are keen to use them, we still lag behind with underpowered heat sources. Although woks have been cheaply and readily available for a while, results are often disappointing, and enthusiasts often use them outdoors and over barbecue charcoal to obtain enough heat.† It's probably a fair bet that as Indian, Chinese and other food types become more popular in the West and the efficiency and healthiness of wok-style cooking becomes more apparent, we can expect to see better designed woks in more kitchens all over the world, along with ways to heat them.

---

* Round-bottomed, thin metal pots also appear in India, South East Asia, Japan, Korea and other cultures that traded with China. Everything that can be said about a wok is equally true of a karahi.

† A recent 'kitchen of the future' designed by Phillips, featured built-in steam ovens, a sous-vide device and an induction heater cast in the bowl shape of the wok bottom and set into the countertop.

CLOCKS AND TIMERS

IT'S WORTH DISTINGUISHING between what one might call *absolute* and *comparative* time. A clock was always necessary in the kitchen of a great house, where cook needed to have supper in the dining room at a particular hour. Most cooks, however, work with comparative time. It doesn't matter how long the madeleines take to cook, it only matters that you can repeat them accurately every time.*

Early recipes specify a hot or a low heat and anything else is moderate. Timing was invariably specified as 'until done'. Experience took the place of thermometer and timer. Where accurate time mattered, cooks improvised more personal timing methods for repeated delicate work. Some early cookbooks revived the monastic tradition of timing things like boiled eggs with Hail Marys.†

Today we are used to the idea that cooking is about temperature and time. When we communicate recipes or instructions, we can specify these things and expect a reasonable amount of repeatability. This is because, since the arrival of controllable ovens, we've standardised cooking temperatures and – because we expect to be able to cook from a recipe, successfully, at the first attempt – the cook now needs to measure absolute time in order to cook. The clock, or a similar absolute timing device, became ubiquitous in the domestic kitchen at the same time as the recipe book.

The hourglass is one of the oldest devices we have for measuring the passage of time. It's unaffected by moisture or heat and can be subdivided into portions of an hour. The egg timer is a smaller version, usually designed to run for three minutes. The simple clockwork timer was a definite improvement – particularly when equipped with an audible alarm – and small portable versions were advertised as 'liberating' devices, as the cook could leave the kitchen and do chores elsewhere in the house.

It was a simple matter to add a small clock to an electric oven and this was soon adapted into a device that could be set with both the duration of cooking and a start time. This meant that a loaf of bread or a casserole would be ready just in time for dinner, but the important change here was how the timer was presented. It was possible for a cook to be out of the house while cooking started in his or her absence.

Today, kitchen appliance designers are increasingly connecting their devices to household networks and the Internet. Ovens, slow cookers, kettles, toasters, fridges and sous-vide devices can be triggered and controlled remotely, by the clock on the cook's mobile phone. Even when cooking traditionally, many of us have grown used to tapping the face of the mobile with floury fingers and yelling 'set timer to 35 minutes'. In the same way as the wristwatch has become redundant in the age of the mobile phone, perhaps the kitchen clock will return to being a quirky wall decoration.

---

* Or that you can 'over' or 'under' cook at will.

† Sounds daft until you consider that a monk, who may have been repeating the same prayer hundreds of times a day, would naturally have lapsed into a standard, or at least habitual, time. A good Hail Mary would be repeatable to fractions of a second. Certainly accurate enough for soft-boiled eggs.

MEASURING JUG

BY NECESSITY CHEFS in large staffed kitchens quickly build up a repertoire of dishes. Cooks have to repeat the same dish many times and learn from experience which timings, temperatures and quantities produce the best results. Domestic cooks usually do not have the time or incentive to develop such knowledge and are generally reliant on written recipes.

Recipe writers in different cultures have, irritatingly, formed opposing camps when it comes to systems of measurement. British recipes initially used imperial weights and volumes, only latterly adopting the metric system that brought them into accordance with the rest of Europe. Dry ingredients, therefore, could be measured in grammes and kilograms and liquids in millilitres and litres. To add an extra touch of logic, one litre of most liquids used in cooking weighs one kilogram.

Of course, the absolute weights and volumes of ingredients are not actually as important as their ratios to each other, so it is also possible – indeed desirable – to express all quantities as either volumes or weights to make such recipes easier to execute and to scale. Professional bakers and brewers, for example, weigh all their ingredients – liquid and solid – and bakers even record their ingredient quantities as percentages.

No one is quite sure why the Americans adopted volume as their standard measure but, over the years, recipes have come to be expressed in 'cups'. Several historians have pointed to the ease of using a cup measure in a remote homestead or the back of a chuck wagon, and those of a more scientific bent say that weight is a less useful measure in the US where certain types of scales (see page 50) vary with altitude. The truth is probably much simpler: if recipes come in cups you don't need jugs or scales.

Whatever the reason for the variation, any home cook wishing to take advantage of recipes from other countries will need a quick and simple way of doing the immensely complex translation and conversion. The measuring jug is simplest, with imperial and metric measurements displayed alongside volumetric markings for a representative selection of dry ingredients.

SPICE RACK

HERBS AND SPICES, some of our rarest and costliest ingredients, need careful storage. Saffron fades and loses potency if exposed to light. Oil-bearing, woody spices like nutmeg and cinnamon weaken if they're not kept cold – preferably below freezing. Ground herbs like ginger or coriander seed will form useless clumps if they're not kept rigorously dry. All should be used promptly. In professional kitchens, things will be stored in appropriate containers, but perhaps the one way you could guarantee to comprehensively bugger up your home collection of seasonings is to store them in clear glass bottles on a little shelf or rack over the cooker.

Think back to the parental spice rack. Its length would be a fair social indicator of income bracket or the number of foreign holidays you'd been able to afford. The popular 'Black Pepper' and 'Herbes de Provence' jars were usually empty while most of the others would, over time, have dulled to a uniform beige. Were it not for the extravagantly lettered labels you'd have trouble distinguishing turmeric from paprika.

Companies dealing in herbs must have been aware of the power of their product in social signalling. The Canadian company Schwartz began supplying herbs and spices in bottles with a moulded collar that fitted into a wooden 'comb'-style rack. This ensured not only that you had to buy their products if you wanted to use the rack, but also that you had to buy enough of them to fill the vacant slots. Even today when we have access to a huge variety of seasonings from all over the globe, this strategy of appealing to the completist and collector in every cook through packaging design proves successful.*

---

* Royal grocer Fortnum & Mason have a range of seasonings packaged in beautiful little paint tins with gorgeously illustrated labels. Each spice is colour coded and numbered to ensure that though your cooking may survive without 'Milled Ancho Chilli', your shelf will be forever incomplete without the brick orange shade and the number 67.

MASALA DABBA

PERHAPS COOKS in Indian families feel less insecure about spices, perhaps they have never felt the need to display them quite so conspicuously. The masala dabba has long been a feature of Indian home kitchens, often passed down the generations as an heirloom. A closely sealed metal tin that keeps out air, moisture and light, it contains smaller canisters that keep the spices apart but give easy access for selection (a single small spoon is usually included).

There are usually seven pots in a dabba* which are filled by the cook. Mine contains turmeric, chilli powder, ground cumin, fenugreek seed, black mustard seed, cardamom and garam masala, but there are infinite combinations depending on the cook, style and region. Some cooks keep one dabba for ground spices and another for whole ones, but always pick a size† that ensures that the spices are used quickly and kept fresh.

Some modern dabbas have individual lids on the pots that supposedly mean the spices will last longer. Not only do lids make the dabba more difficult to use, but I've always felt they would somehow be an admission that I was failing to get through enough spices.

Since spice racks first appeared in domestic kitchens they have proved a bellwether of culinary influence. Today, for example, a spice rack might contain ras al hanout, Chinese five spice, half a dozen different chillies, galangal, tamarind, amchoor (dried mango powder) and sansho pepper. Food writers and other 'experts' have often poured scorn on the naff spice rack, but in truth no single kitchen item is a more heartening symbol of the adventurousness of domestic cooks and the growing diversity of our home menus. For a while, when our culinary horizons stretched no further than the Mediterranean, perhaps we might have aspired to pop out into the kitchen garden and gather fresh herbs. Now our repertoires have become so international, we're once again relying on our spice and dried herb collections and, pleasingly, many Western kitchens have a masala dabba of their own.

---

* Seven circular pots of the same size will tessellate perfectly in a larger circle. If a dabba is to have more than seven, then the central pot must be of a different, larger diameter.

† Diameters are usually between 18 and 30 centimetres (7 and 12 inches).

SALAD SPINNER

FOR CENTURIES European cooks had regarded 'salads' with justifiable distrust. Ground-growing crops, particularly those grown in market gardens near to cities, were kept fertile by liberal applications of the city's own waste products. 'Night soil' was collected in carts, driven to the outskirts and spread out over the fields. There couldn't really have been a surer way of picking up an intestinal bug than eating uncooked ground-plants like lettuce. Cooks who did use salad plants washed them carefully and then whirled them round in a cloth or a basket, using centrifugal force to drive off the water.

Hand-cranked or electrically driven 'spin' dryers for clothes had been around since the 1800s, so it's testament to the long-lasting human antipathy to salad that the salad spinner wasn't actually patented until 1971 when Moulinex, the serial innovators of Gallic gadgetry, launched a basket that spun in a bowl, powered by a hand-driven gear system.

This was a boon to cooks and salad eaters alike. Whipping a wet cloth full of leaves around the kitchen was both damp and ineffective, and there are few things more guaranteed to induce misery than a damp salad. Beyond its mere fitness for purpose, the new gadget was propelled to success in the United States where a mania for healthy, vegetable-based eating was developing.

Designs for salad spinners have changed little from the first patents and though they've inspired large-scale electric washers in commercial kitchens where ultraviolet light is also used as an additional antibacterial precaution, these seem to be, as yet, considered *de trop* in the home.

SILICONE SPATULA

'SILICONE RUBBER'[*] was developed in the 1940s by US companies searching for electrical insulators. The material could be set or cured to many different textures but all were flexible, tough, heat-resistant and food-safe. Initially silicone rubber was used inside other more complex appliances – the seals on fridge or cooker doors, cable gaskets on kettles and mixers – but it was the silicone spatula that brought the material most directly into the grateful hands of cooks everywhere.

There had always been scrapers[†] in the kitchen. It didn't take much ingenuity to reshape an old wooden spoon, the better to winkle stuff out of remote corners of pots and jars. But silicone rubber – non-stick, inert and totally flexible – fitted every vessel perfectly, scraping jam, lard, gravy, cake batter and mayonnaise cleanly from whatever corner they lurked in jars, bowls and even hot pans. The silicone spatula wasn't just an incredibly simple object, it was a genuine improvement on everything that had gone before in a way that daily proved its worth. This was no gimmicky gadget. Waste was reduced. Pots were as clean as if they'd been licked by children.[‡]

Unlike almost every other kitchen 'improvement' it's impossible to find a credible body of resistance to the wonder that is the silicone spatula.[§] In fact the only negative thing anyone can think of to say about it is that it is marginally less awesome than the spoonula,[¶] a more recent development that combines the scraping and lifting utility of the spatula with the dished scooping profile of a serving spoon.[**]

---

[*] It should more accurately be called polysiloxane. A polymer made of alternating Si and O atoms.

[†] There is much controversy over the word 'spatula'. In American usage a spatula – from the ancient Greek *spathe*, meaning broad blade – is the device used for flipping things in frying pans, what the British sometimes refer to as a 'fish slice'. The silicon rubber 'spatula' in its simplest form is more properly a scraper.

[‡] It is arguable that the only people who didn't benefit from the silicone spatula were the eager pot lickers.

[§] See also Microplane grater, page 33.

[¶] Awful, I know, but better than Spatoon.

[**] Nobody has been able to explain quite why, but the spoonula even improves mashed potato. When used to beat butter or cream into the mash before serving, it somehow renders it smooth and light without breaking up the cells and making it gloopy or starchy. Try it, I implore you.

EGG CUP AND CODDLER

IN COMMERCIAL KITCHENS poaching or hard-boiling eggs is a common task, with eggs cooked in large batches and often held at temperature. The single egg is rarely regarded as a meal or even a course by itself and is usually used as an ingredient in or a garnish for another dish. But at home one or two eggs are an ideal and convenient meal for a single person. Preparing a couple of eggs for oneself is almost the definition of pleasurable, low-stress, comforting cooking, which is why so many of the appliances concerned with small-scale egg cookery appear simultaneously with domestic rather than commercial kitchens.

Designer Willhelm Wagenfeld trained at the Bauhaus and in 1933, while working as a designer with the Jenaer Glas company, he created the 'No 1' egg coddler. This was made with the same borosilicate glass then being used to make huge electric lamps for factories and laboratory equipment. The three pieces clip together, are easy to clean and enable anyone with access to boiling water to improve on the simple boiling of an egg in its shell. The coddler has no place in the professional kitchen; it's a purely domestic object on a wonderfully humane scale – as Wagenfeld put it, 'cheap enough for the poor and good enough for the rich'. It's no wonder that it can be found on pedestals in design museums around the world.

While many nations eat their boiled eggs manually, by cracking and peeling, it is a proud British tradition to cook the egg soft and to dip toasted bread 'soldiers' into the yolk. To this end we have developed the egg cup, which presents the egg perfectly for decapitation and dippage. Cooking the egg to the ideal point of softness can be difficult,* so these cups are equipped with insulated covers. These retain the heat inside the egg, allowing it to 'cook on' if it's been slightly underdone.

---

*　It is repeatedly rumoured that a member of the British Royal family has seven eggs prepared for him every morning, cooked for slightly different times so that one will be in the perfect state for dipping. It is important to note that the Palace has emphatically denied that this is true. Personally, if I were heir to the throne, I'd have nine cooked … and served to me in bed.

PRESSURE COOKER

INVENTED IN FRANCE in 1679, the pressure cooker began life as a strictly professional piece of cooking equipment.* It was large, complicated, often dangerous (early models were liable to explode) and its best use was in rendering cheap and challenging materials edible. Pressure cookers were useful for feeding hospital inmates, soldiers, students, servants or the occupants of any large institution where economy was important. It was too coarse a tool for fine and delicate cooking and usually too large to be relevant to ordinary families.

The first domestic-sized pressure cookers became available in the 1930s. They were still complex to operate and prone to terrifying accidents, but they were sold to householders through two compelling benefits: health and thrift. Fad diets are often built around a particular technology with promises that extra nutrients can be obtained through various processes; the pressure cooker had already proved itself capable of this.

In 1912 the term 'vitamin' was first coined and with it came a wide public fascination with their effects on health and wellbeing. Because the pressure cooker worked fast – using high-temperature steam and in a very obviously sealed environment – and perhaps also because it looked like a piece of scientific equipment, it was easy to believe that it preserved these vital dietary elements. In many cases this was enough of an attraction to overcome the householder's justifiable fear of having such an item in the kitchen.

Once pressure cookers became cheaper and more widely available their second benefit of fuel efficiency ensured that they spread worldwide. In 1959 Hawkins Cookers Ltd began manufacturing pressure cookers in India where they immediately became enormously successful.† Pressure cookers remain strangely polarising devices. Those who believe in their powers and invest the time to learn to operate and trust them are rewarded with excellent results. Yet a sizeable part of the public still regard them with the same wariness they would a hand grenade – even though modern pressure cookers, laden with safety features, are among the safest tools we have. They are still not so widely accepted that recipe books routinely list pressure cooking instructions, and so there is a large enough canon of specialist cookbooks and websites to consider the device a cult, if not actually a full-blown religion.

---

* When Denis Papin invented the 'steam digester', it was intended to be used to feed the poor with broth extracted from otherwise waste bones. Obviously poor people were not expected to own digesters, but workhouses and soup kitchens could.

† An annual Brand Trust Report found the Hawkins pressure cooker to be India's most trusted kitchen appliance in 2015.

ON
APPLIANCES

K EY TO THE EVOLUTION of the modern kitchen has been the arrival of services and appliances, many of which created radical change.

Since the earliest development of cities, water has been piped or pumped to public standpipes from where it would be collected by servants or householders. If we wonder today how one could survive using only as much water as one could carry, we should probably also consider that, until the arrival of mains sewerage in mid-Victorian London, disposal of waste was such an issue that lower consumption was probably a benefit. In 1854 Sir John Snow, Queen Victoria's personal physician, was able to stem a cholera outbreak in Golden Square, Soho, by removing the handle of the local water pump.

Some grand houses might have had a private pump in the yard but, even here, water was such a precious commodity that sand was more commonly used to 'wash up' pots and crockery.

Piped mains water, once it arrived, was brought into the house at the closest point to the main. In Victorian middle-class terraced housing and villas, developers usually located the main alongside the sewer under the street in front of the houses. Water appeared through a single tap often sited in the basement, and a great deal of servants' time was taken up in heating it and carrying it around the house. In working-class terraces and courts, the main often rose in the back yard or side passage – often where the communal pump had been located. In working-class terraces a small 'scullery' at the back of the house was where water arrived and washing was done, but any heating of food would still have taken place in the main living room where the fire supplied heat.

Perhaps this is why 'the kitchen sink' is a more important symbol of the kitchen than the hearth or stove. In homes without servants that pre-dated washing machines and dishwashers, the sink was the main workstation of the housewife. Washing clothes, washing dishes and even preparing food, before packaging made it so clean, all took place at the sink. It's therefore not surprising that in most kitchens the sink takes pride of place at the window, where there was access to light. Even modern kitchens where, thanks to the automatic dishwasher, nobody seems to stand at the sink any longer than the time it takes to fill a kettle, are still designed around this anachronism.

Kitchen ranges were first made in the 18th century, simple designs that enclosed the domestic fire and sometimes included a built-in water boiling tank. These were expensive items that could only be afforded by the rich, while working-class, particularly urban, families still relied heavily on hot food bought from shops or street vendors. By the 19th century some domestic fireplaces were fitted with adaptations for cooking. These hybrid arrangements looked like a regular cast iron fire surround, but might have had a shelf for a pot or kettle that swung in from the side, a small water tank (this would need to be filled from a jug) or, occasionally, a small grill that could be flipped over the coals. There might have been a hook from which to suspend a kettle or even a clockwork roasting 'jack', but for most, arrangements were more makeshift*.

Gas manufacture began in England at the beginning of the 19th century and was initially used for street lighting. In some cities gas supply was a municipal arrangement; in others it was run by monopolistic gas generation companies, and by the end of the century these were delivering gas to private homes for lighting, heating and cooking. Gas mains usually ran close to water mains and gas usually entered the house close to the location of water and sewerage. As a result, the location of a 'kitchen' within the building was the obvious solution.

---

* 'There was something in front of the fire, too, that would have been inviting to a hungry man, if it had been in a different stage of cooking. It was a small bit of pork suspended from the kettle-hanger by a string passed through a large door-key, in a way known to primitive housekeepers unpossessed of jacks. But the pork had been hung at the farthest extremity of the hanger, apparently to prevent the roasting from proceeding too rapidly during the owner's absence. The old staring simpleton had hot meat for his supper, then? thought Dunstan. People had always said he lived on mouldy bread, on purpose to check his appetite. But where could he be at this time, and on such an evening, leaving his supper in this stage of preparation, and his door unfastened?' George Eliot, *Silas Marner* (1861).

By the 1920s we start to see gas-fired combination stoves of the sort we might recognise today – a small box oven topped with several controllable rings at waist level. Even these were restricted to middle-class homes. A brief perusal of any Patrick Hamilton novel or one of George Orwell's investigative odysseys reveals that the urban poor and bedsit dwellers shared a gas ring on each landing or made toast over the single bar of the electric fire until after the Second World War.

The first electric stove was unveiled at an Electrical Fair at the Crystal Palace in 1891 and a similar device appeared at the Chicago World's Fair in 1893; the 'General Electric Range' was mass produced in 1905. In that same year Australian David Curle Smith* patented the Kalgoorlie Stove, the first to use the format that became the worldwide standard of an oven, with a grill above it and a set of burner rings on top.

Across the industrialised world the provision of gas and electricity utilities to urban centres was fast becoming an important and lucrative business. Companies competed for franchises and in some places governments nationalised production; everywhere, increased domestic use was seen as the key to increased profits. Gas and electricity companies competed aggressively to persuade housewives of all classes to adopt their appliances. In some places, a gas or electric cooker could be offered free as an incentive to buy into the supply; in others the newly fashionable 'hire purchase' arrangements meant that cost was less of a problem for even the poorest families.

Advertising was ferocious – almost to the point of propaganda – with gas being sold on the grounds of cheapness and efficiency and electricity being pushed as the more sophisticated and cleaner option. At other levels stories were promulgated that gas was lethal and electricity uncontrollable. Both gas and electricity companies sponsored magazines, recipe books, programmes on radio and the

*   Curle Smith's wife Nora Murdoch wrote a cookbook, *Thermo-Electrical Cooking Made Easy* (1907), to help promote her husband's electric cooker. Her family has continued to be extraordinarily successful in publishing and other media across the world right up to the present day.

new 'television' and even had teams of uniformed 'trainers' who would go into ordinary people's homes to teach them how to get the best out of their new appliances.*

Refrigeration devices had long had industrial and commercial applications, but it took them a surprisingly long time to move into the domestic setting. Though insulated enclosures using naturally occurring ice had been used for centuries, it was James Harrison who patented the first commercially practical 'vapour-compression' regfrigeration unit in Australia in 1856. This made the exportation of frozen meat or long storage of products like beer financially viable, but the equipment was too large to find a place in a normal home. The first domestic 'fridges' from companies like Kelvinator, Frigidaire and Electrolux comprised an insulated coldbox in the kitchen connected to more heavy plant in a basement or outside shed. These were considered practical in large American houses, but it was the arrival of a self-contained unit from General Electric in 1927 that made domestic refrigeration a real possibility in other countries. In places like Australia where heat was a serious consideration (and chilled beer a basic human right), fridges quickly gained popularity while in Britain things took much longer.

British homes had long been planned with a built-in larder. This would be a thick, walled cupboard, usually built against the colder north-facing wall and with ventilation to the outside. Many were equipped with a marble or tiled shelf that 'held' the cold and most could be counted on reliably to remain at two or three degrees colder than the rest of the house. In poorer homes, meat, cheese or milk could be kept longer by storing them on a window sill; some householders built a wire mesh 'meat safe' outside a kitchen window, where food could be kept cold and not be interfered with by passers-by or inquisitive wildlife.

---

* Perhaps most famous of these trainers was a young woman who worked for the South Western Electricity Board, driving around the City of Bath in a Ford Popular, demonstrating the effectiveness of home electric ovens. Mary Berry continues her successful career in cookery education today.

It's indicative of the relative lack of importance of the fridge to British cooks* that in his 1965 *Action Cookbook* the great Len Deighton includes an entire chapter called 'Who Needs a Refrigerator?', in which he rails against its tendency to irreparably spoil Camembert and its inability to manufacture enough ice for a decent-sized party.

The problem of keeping food warm from the kitchen to the table has always been with us. Many gadgets in the form of insulated containers or heated plates† had been successfully used, and the chafing dish remained perennially useful, but it was the L.G. Hawkins‡ company who launched the first 'heated sideboard' in 1931. This could keep food warm for ages, but still required someone – and in this context we can imagine 'staff' – to move the food from the kitchen to the holding cabinet. History does not record which genius first thought to put the cabinet on wheels, but in 1953 the Hostess Trolley was born.

---

* Elizabeth David had, as she did in all things, strong opinions about refrigerators. In an article she contributed to *The Kitchen Book* in 1977, she wanted it banished from the kitchen: 'Outside the kitchen is my refrigerator and there it will stay. I keep it at the lowest temperature, about 4°C. I'm still amazed at the way so-called model kitchens have refrigerators next to the cooking stove. This seems to me almost as mad as having a wine rack above it. Then, failing a separate larder, there would be a second and fairly large refrigerator to be used for the cool storage of a variety of commodities such as coffee beans, spices, butter, cheese and eggs, which benefit from a constant temperature of say 10°C.'

† One useful 17th-century device was a heated plate, usually used for game, in which a lead jacket was moulded onto the bottom of a ceramic plate. This could be filled through a spout with boiling water, which meant the gravy wouldn't congeal as the butler took the long walk up the stairs and along the East Wing Gallery.

‡ Based in Hastings, L.G. Hawkins was responsible for many early electrical appliances, including the automatic tea maker and the hand-held hair dryer. Perhaps their greatest commercial success, though, was the manufacture and supply of pressure cookers (known as 'Hawkins cookers') to India (see page 109).

The name says it all. The trolley solved the problem of the cook without staff who needed to cater for social occasions – in effect the lower middle-class housewife, navigating the social shark-pool of the dinner party. The trolley was designed to hold the food in Pyrex dishes, in an insulated cupboard or on a hotplate top. The trolley could be loaded in the afternoon, wheeled into the dining room and set up next to the table. The hostess, it was imagined, would repair to her chiffon-trimmed dressing table and prepare herself, greet her guests and have a cocktail or two before serving hot food to applause and social acclaim. Sure, the food may by this point have achieved the texture of a school dinner or canteen lunch, but there was at least the momentary illusion that the hostess had not personally sweated over the preparation; a socially sustainable, if factually false, severing of the connection between cooking and serving.

This is how a great deal of advertising presented the Hostess trolley, with photographs of impossibly elegant women serving peas that somehow didn't look like they'd spent the afternoon on life-support in a sauna of gravy steam. It may be one of the unspoken tragedies of the era that, in spite of the aspirational market* into which they were sold, very few hostess trolleys were ever used for dinner parties. They did, though, serve thousands of family Sunday lunches, Christmas dinners and, amongst Jewish families keeping kosher, an acceptably hot lunch on the Sabbath.

The first patent for a dishwasher was granted to a man called Joel Houghton. His device operated by splashing water ineffectually onto the dirty dishes. The second, which was distinguished by the fact that it actually worked, was invented by a woman. Please insert your own joke here if you wish. I'm not going near it.

---

* I confess that I grew up in a house with a hostess trolley and I can't remember it ever having been used. Like many of my generation, I remember the hostess trolley best as the top prize on game shows. For the growing mass audiences of commercial TV channels, the hostess trolley briefly occupied a misty peak of social aspiration, the ultimate consumer good imaginable.

Josephine Garis Cochrane was a wealthy socialite who often entertained and worried about keeping the costly tableware she used at parties out of the clumsy hands of servants.

When her husband, a Democrat politician, died leaving her substantial debts, she built the first prototype machine in a garden shed with the part-time help of a local railroad engineer called George Butters. Unlike previous attempts, the 'Cochrane' used jets of hot soapy water instead of brushes and held the dishes safe in a rotating custom-made wire frame. The hand-cranked machine was patented in 1886.* The dishwasher was an immediate success with large catering establishments and hospitals – most of which also had large suites of standard-sized matching china and appreciated the sterilising effects of very hot water,† but there was little imaginable use for it in the home.

In the post-war American consumer boom, washing dishes remained the last truly unpleasant kitchen chore that had yet to be eased by technology. With homes now routinely plumbed with a good supply of hot water and mains electricity effectively ubiquitous, it was the perfect time for the domestic dishwasher to come into its own. The first versions were, like washing machines, free-standing appliances that commanded extremely high prices. They took off in the affluent US, but in other parts of the world, particularly Europe, they were still seen as somehow decadent, lazy or effete. It was only in the 1970s, when dishwashers were made to be installed in fashionable fitted kitchens and prices dropped, that they began to approach ubiquity.

---

* On the strength of her invention Cochrane founded the Garis-Cochrane Manufacturing Company in a disused schoolhouse. The company was bought by Hobart in 1916 (still the main manufacturer of commercial dishwashers), which later became KitchenAid ... which was bought by Whirlpool. Though this is probably a pretty standard corporate genealogy, it's rather lovely to think of Cochrane in her garden shed, the founding mother of a huge amount of the kitchen appliance industry.

† Garis-Cochrane was granted a patent for an electrically driven version of the machine in 1900.

WOODEN SPOON

THE WOODEN SPOON is one of our oldest kitchen implements, with recorded examples going back to the Paleolithic era. Whittling wood or bone into a shape that carries wet food to the mouth is such a simple and obvious thing to do that we can almost regard it as innate. Wood is easy to work, so knocking out a spoon or two isn't difficult, but we don't carve our own any more so why do wooden spoons persist when we have so many other materials available to us?

Unlike metal, wood conducts almost no heat. You can stir a simmering sauce for days with a wooden spoon and the handle will never burn you. You can taste something from a wooden spoon without burning your lips. As wood is softer than copper, tin or Teflon, a wooden spoon will never damage the linings of expensive pans. Best of all, a wooden spoon improves with age. Every chip, burn or stain adds to its character and a small pot holding a selection of well-loved spoons is regarded as almost symbolic of the contented home cook. It's certainly become 'iconic' enough to be the cover image of countless cookbooks.

Today, in a bizarre reversal of history, spoon carving has regained popularity. There must be something in the rustic simplicity of producing such an honest domestic object by hand that appeals to the crowded mind of the busy young hipster. In truth, I've never found a handcrafted spoon that even begins to match the utility of the simplest mass-produced one but, as with so much that is romantically useless in the modern kitchen, perhaps I'm missing the point.

Although wooden spoons are as easy to keep clean as any others,* environmental health legislation has taken against them in many jurisdictions. Metal or silicon spoons are thought easier to keep sterile. For this reason the wooden spoon looks likely to survive only in a domestic setting, perhaps where the patina of history and a strong family backstory can be better appreciated.

---

* Put through the dishwasher and allow to dry naturally, standing upright. The spoons. Not you.

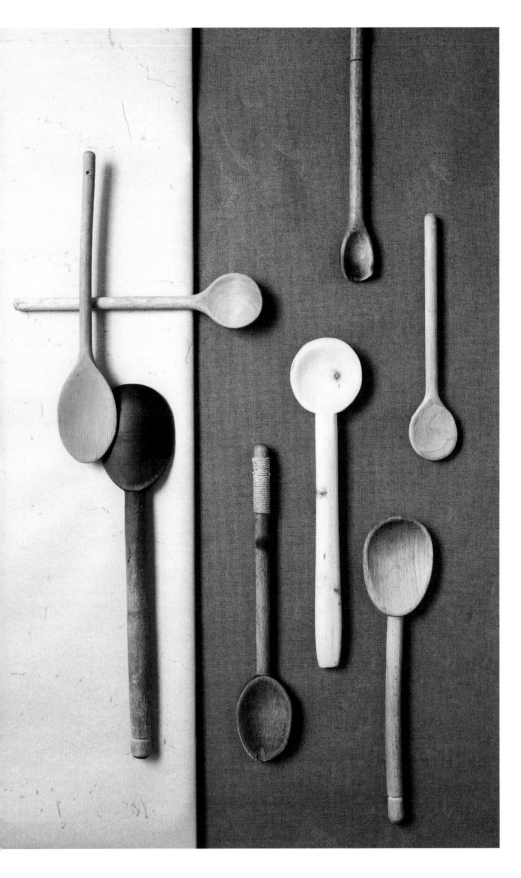

SPRINGFORM BAKING TIN

IT'S HARD TO PIN DOWN exactly where the term 'tinker' comes from. *Tincar* is a Sanskrit word for borax, which is used as flux in soldering, and itinerant metal workers were called 'tinklers' in Medieval England. It certainly seems to have been associated with light-metal work for a very long time. Though skilled metalworkers might possibly have found permanent positions in factories after the Industrial Revolution, they would originally have got much more work by travelling regular routes where they could do repairs on farms, in workshops and, importantly, in kitchens.

As a result, the kitchen in a farm or large country house would have had quite a lot of sheet steel, copper or iron utensils, many of which had been custom-built to the designs of the head cook or utilising the ingenuity of the tinsmith.

Cake tins with removable bases were a simple but brilliant idea that would have risen naturally from the needs of the baker and the way a basic baking tin was constructed. Leaving the base loose, rather than soldering it firmly in place, would have helped the cook to pop out a cake or pie.

No one knows who first made a cake pan with an expanding collar to make the process even simpler. There had been wooden pie moulds that split open along a hinge, but the wide clip that makes what we universally refer to today as a 'springform'* can't be credited to any individual or company.

The springform not only made it easier to turn the cake out, but also marked a degree of standardisation in domestic bakeware. Homeowners were getting used to cooking without servants. They needed recipes and recipes meant that weights, measures, temperatures and times had to be standardised and repeatable. It doesn't really matter who made the first 9-inch 'springform' because it soon became the basic standard measurement in domestic cake-making.

---

* Springform doesn't appear to be registered as a trademark in any of the major jurisdictions and is used profligately by many bakeware manufacturers.

CAST-IRON SKILLET

SURE, THEY FRY EGGS over the fire in cowboy movies but you'd sure grow tired of holdin' that heavy pan over the flames, pard'ner. A pot sits well in a fire or propped among the coals, but a skillet, wide and shallow, is really designed for use on a more structured range or stove. There had been bakestones, griddles and girdle plates before, but the cast-iron skillet opened up a whole new area of cooking. For the first time, searing and shallow frying of more delicate proteins became available to all.

Cast iron is great for holding heat, so it tends to even out the temperature as a heat source rises and falls and, though it's prone to hot spots if not moved around on the stove, it's a remarkably forgiving utensil. Very few things will give a seared outer crust to a steak as well as a preheated, nearly dry skillet. At lower temperatures, nothing will hold the oil at the perfect point for fried chicken quite so well or so long. Skillets are cast in sand moulds, which give the characteristic pitted surface to the outside. Historically, the inside of a skillet would then be polished or machined to create an entirely smooth cooking surface. Today, most cookware manufacturers don't bother with this final step, which means that old skillets found in junk shops and car boot sales can often be superior.

With constant use and care, the bottom of the skillet will build up a seasoning* layer of polymerized fat which bonds to the metal and forms an effectively 'non-stick' surface. This can be damaged by insensitive washing† or rough handling, which explains why a good skillet was so treasured and so jealously protected by many cooks.

The development of enamel coating to cast-iron cookware meant that the skillet could be easier to take care of and, as new materials like aluminium or stainless steel became popular, the old skillet fell out of fashion to be replaced by the more modern frying pan.

Cast iron has always had its adherents though. In the American Deep South, the skillet has never dropped out of daily use, and many keen cooks have kept the faith, seasoning and polishing a skillet even when it stays at the back of the cupboard for months at a time.

Today, cast iron is achieving a certain hipster cachet, with small forges run by men with beards making fantastic new skillets at very high prices. It's worth noting though, that all the best forges continue to recondition old skillets, which seem to retain even more spirit and are somehow even more valued.

---

* To season your pan, put it in the oven on full heat, add a splash of neutral oil and paint it carefully around the hot surface with wadded kitchen towel. Allow the pan to cool naturally in the oven with the heat turned off. After each subsequent use, clean out the pan carefully, heat it until it begins to smoke and then run an oil-soaked cloth over the inside.

† The seasoning layer is surprisingly robust. Tough, cooked-on remains can be scrubbed off with coarse salt. It's perfectly OK to clean out your pan with a plastic brush or scouring pad and even a little soap. Just dry it immediately afterwards, re-season a little if necessary and NEVER leave it to soak.

ELECTRIC RICE COOKER

RICE IS THE MOST COMMONLY CONSUMED dietary staple on the planet but it's not easy to cook well. Overcooked it becomes a sloppy porridge; undercooked it's difficult to digest. It's easy to burn it or stick it to the pan. And the places where rice is most commonly cooked have been the last reached by gas or electricity. It's unsurprising, then, that the purpose-built, self-contained rice cooker took so long to be invented, and perhaps even less surprising that once it was, it spread with incredible speed across the world.

The basic principle of the rice cooker is simple. A measured quantity of rice and water goes into an electrically heated pot which is sealed. As the heat is applied, the temperature of the water rises to boiling. The steam produced cooks the rice, which absorbs moisture until it's perfectly cooked and dry. The moment the last water has been absorbed, the heat is no longer absorbed in evaporating it and the temperature of the system begins to rise rapidly, causing a simple thermostat to cut off the power. Though there had been earlier experiments with electrically heated rice pots it wasn't until 1956 that the first sealed 'automatic' rice cooker – the first that actually 'decided' when the rice was ready – was put on sale in Japan. Within four years there were automatic rice cookers in half the homes in the country.

In the years since, rice cookers have spread all over the world. There have been simple technological advances such as timers, induction elements and non-stick coating, but also some astonishingly 'space age' science. Some of the most cutting-edge Japanese electronic technology, including 'fuzzy logic' computer control, were rushed to market as automatic rice cookers became ubiquitous. This ensured more consistent cooking in all conditions and allowed functions like programming of cooking times, pre-selection of texture preferences, conditioning and holding cycles.

As in any other market, less functional and more aesthetic considerations also led to interesting variations in design. In countries where high-status rice cooking pots had historically been made of copper or ceramic, expensive luxury rice cookers were designed to include these materials.

In recent years some of the technology of the rice cooker has been combined with the principles of the Crock-Pot and the pressure cooker to create the 'Instant Pot', a proprietary self-contained cooking pot with a wider range of functions.

OLIVE OIL JUG

THE OLIVE OIL JUG IS ONE of the ceremonial objects of the British middle-class kitchen. There is a simple and intriguing reason for this, based in what has become, by constant repetition, a widely disseminated myth about its history.

Take a moment to Google the words 'Elizabeth David Ears Olive Oil Boots' and you'll link to the hundreds of reputable writers and bloggers who have repeated the story: 'Until Elizabeth David championed it in the late 1950s, the only place you could buy olive oil in the UK was Boots the Chemist where it was sold for cleaning wax out of your ears'.

This is held as gospel truth by food lovers all over the country, and if you want to start a fistfight among the floaty shawls of a bunch of food writers, just try questioning the perceived wisdom.

But the truth is quite different. Olive oil is listed in the BPC* and yes, high-street chemists still sell it for cleaning ears. But British recipe books that pre-date the likes of Mrs Beeton and Hannah Glasse, suggested olive oil as an ingredient. Sydney Smith recommended it in poems.† 'Oil of Lucca' was certainly available in London at the time of Samuel Pepys (although he didn't record whether he buried any during the Great Fire along with his Parmesan cheese). In the 14th century 'oyle de olive' is prescribed to 'fry fysshe' in the 'Forme of Cury', the first known cookbook written in English. In her writing, Saint David herself actually suggests obtaining olive oil from the many Italian or Spanish importers in Soho.

Any rediscovery or popularisation of olive oil as an ingredient can only have been a good thing, given that the alternatives in the British larder were butter for the rich and recovered animal fat drippings for the poor, but it is always interesting when cooks choose to put a particular ingredient on display rather than keeping it in some discreet and serviceable container out of sight.

Largely through David's writing, the liberal use of olive oil became an important indicator that a cook was broad-minded, cosmopolitan and sophisticated. The olive oil jug on the kitchen counter is part of the ritual altar suite of the true believer, along with the garlic pot and the jar full of wooden spoons.‡

---

* The British Pharmaceutical Codex, the '… book of reference for pharmacists and medical practitioners … on all drugs and medicines in common use throughout the British Empire (including those in the British Pharmacopoeia) … and a book of standards for drugs and preparations not included in the British Pharmacopoeia.'

† In an 1839 letter to Lady Holland, Sydney Smith shares his recipe for salad dressing using olive oil: 'Of mordant mustard add a single spoon … Four times the spoon with oil of Lucca crown'.

‡ A small jug sometimes forms half of an oil and vinegar 'cruet' – a refinement from hotel tables on package holidays which was brought to the British table by post-war travellers. Freshly made oil and vinegar dressing on a 'crisp green salad' (always eaten separately to the main course) was as important a ritual of the Mediterranean enthusiast's orthodoxy as 'cheese before dessert' or the banishment of fish knives.

SLOW COOKER

IN MANY PARTS of the world, when a family without an oven wanted hot food they would assemble the dish in a clay pot, usually tie it closed with an identifying piece of cloth and then leave it at the local bakery on their way to work in the morning. For a small payment, the baker, who would already have finished the day's baking, would put the collected pots into his oven as it cooled over the day. The food would slow-cook and in the evening, just as the baker needed to relight his oven, the family could pick up their dish, fully cooked, in time for dinner.

Dishes slow-cooked while the cook is at work are so often the triggers for happy nostalgia. This is, in a way, the story behind the Crock-Pot, the popular cooking trend of the 1970s. In 1936 Irving Nachumsohn* applied for the first US patent for an electrical home slow-cooking pot. He fondly remembered a recipe from his mother, an orthodox Jew from Lithuania, for 'cholent'. This is a bean and potato stew that can be brought to the boil on Friday and then stored in the cooling oven where it continues to 'cook' in the residual heat until it is eaten as lunch on the Sabbath. Thus it makes a hot meal while complying with rules forbidding cooking on the holy day.

Nachumsohn's invention, the 'Naxon Beanery All-Purpose Cooker', was a heavy stoneware pot, suspended in an enclosure over an electrical heating element and topped with a lid. The design barely changed in nearly 80 years, though it was renamed the 'Crock-Pot' when the company was taken over in 1971. The electrical element heats the food[†] and then switches to a lower setting that maintains it at just below boiling point. The lid, sometimes glass, sits in a grooved lip on the pot, forming a seal that prevents water vapour from escaping. Once set in action, the slow cooker ensures that the food cannot burn or lose any moisture.[‡]

The United States in the 1970s, when women were returning to full-time work in large numbers, was the perfect environment for success. The advantage of being able to cook for the family 'while at work' was heavily promoted to a new generation of women struggling with 'having it all'. Because the ceramic pot could be lifted out and transported, Crock-Pot meals also became defining staples of family reunions, pot-luck suppers and church picnics. Concentration on speed and convenience, though, meant that many published Crock-Pot recipes featured ingredients like canned mushroom soup or freeze-dried onion soup mix as short cuts.

Along with the pressure cooker, the slow cooker has achieved a sort of cult status outside of the mainstream of food media. Regular recipe books almost never give instructions for using slow or pressure cookers, but a vast body of specialist books, websites, Pinterest boards and user groups has grown up.

---

*   Some sources refer to Nachumsohn's anglicised name, Naxon.

†   You can speed up the process by adding preheated ingredients to the pot.

‡   The original slow cooker had a single knob to control temperature manually. Modern versions may have digital timers and programmers, and a probe to measure the internal temperature of the food.

EGG POACHER

PROFESSIONALS POACH THEIR EGGS in open water, making the egg into a sort of spherical capsule. Strictly an egg is 'poached' when the yolk and albumen are fully immersed and in contact with water. The egg 'poacher' pan suspends the eggs in greased cups in a bath of steam* – so it should more correctly be called a steamer.

If you crack an egg into a saucer you will notice that it has 'two' whites. A portion of the white has a defined shape, as if enclosed in a clear sac, while another portion is entirely liquid. In a fresh egg there is very little of the latter liquid component, but if an egg is stored for a long time, more and more of the white changes to this watery consistency.

When you poach an egg the more solid white cooks well while the thin stuff floats off wildly into the poaching water. In a large kitchen with a large turnover of good-quality, fresh eggs, it's easy to poach them properly; whereas, in the domestic kitchen where eggs are used in smaller numbers over a longer period of time, results would more often than not be disappointing. So at home, the 'egg-poacher pan', which contains and cooks all the white evenly, will actually give a better result more of the time.

Perhaps the single greatest advantage of the poacher pan, though, is the shape it gives the finished eggs. It sets them neatly as a dome with a flat bottom, a shape that could have been designed to fit on a slice of toast. It is no coincidence that the poacher is popular in countries where packaged sliced bread is the norm[†] – the UK, US and Australia – and where the coddler (see page 106) is an exotic thing rarely seen.

---

[*] This is distinct from the coddled egg (see page 106) in which the egg is steamed but in a closed container rather than an open mould. Many people think these distinctions are too fine to be important. They are probably right.

[†] See Bread bin, page 156.

BREVILLE SANDWICH TOASTER

IN URBAN WORKING-CLASS homes during the Industrial Revolution there would rarely have been a kitchen in the recognisable sense. Water may have been brought in from a communal pump, food was often bought precooked from street vendors and any 'cooking ' in the home would have taken place at the hearth. A pot could be hung from a pot-hook, you could toast bread with a suitable fork, you might be able to get a small pan over the coals to fry up a bit of bacon … or you might be the proud owner of a 'pie iron'. The pie iron looked much like the modern waffle maker, but enabled you to take a couple of slices of bread, clamp them round a filling, close the iron and thrust it into the coals to 'bake' a simulacrum of a pie.

The 'pie iron' survives to this day among campers and keen outdoorsy people. In the home it evolved, first to a smaller version that could be used on a gas or electric stove, and then in 1974 into an electrically powered appliance, the mighty 'Breville Snack and Sandwich Toaster'.

The Breville Company, based in Melbourne, had been making electrical equipment since before the Second World War and mine-detecting equipment during it. Witnessing the beginnings of a post-war boom, John O'Brien, son of the company's founder, launched a Research and Development Centre that rapidly became a global centre of excellence for small electrical appliances.[*] According to the creation myth, O'Brien noticed that his children loved 'Jaffles',[†] but sometimes burned themselves when the hot filling squirted out uncontrollably. O'Brien's solution was a heated press that sealed the sandwich and cut it diagonally.

The toasted sandwich maker became popular all over the world, particularly with children. For a whole generation, making a 'toastie' was often the first experience of cooking for yourself. In a strangely circular way, it was also popular with students and others living in accommodation without kitchens – a cheap and simple appliance that could create a whole hot meal without any other equipment.

[*] Breville have over 100 patents for kitchen appliances, including juicers, electric woks, coffee machines and breadmakers. Today they are one of the largest industrial design divisions in Australia.

[†] There was a craze in Australia in the early 1950s for 'Jaffles' – sandwiches toasted in a patented circular 'Jaffle iron'. A favourite filling was savoury mince.

PRESERVING JAR

FRENCHMAN NICOLAS APPERT[*] is credited with the invention of 'canning' for food preservation. He discovered a way of hermetically sealing food into glass jars with a cork and wax and then, in a water bath, raising the temperature until the food cooked through. In a way he was lucky. His process effectively pasteurised the food – even though Pasteur himself didn't discover the idea until 1846.

Appert's process evolved into modern canning – using metal containers[†] – but on a domestic scale cooks continued to preserve in reusable glass jars. There were several patents for the idea and different companies achieved dominance in different markets – Kilner in the UK, Mason in the United States and the Vacola jar in Australia – but all worked on the same beautifully simple principle.

The raw food is placed in the jar with a little airspace above it and a lid with a rubber seal is loosely applied. Using a water bath the whole jar is heated to a point at which the food is cooked through and held for long enough for bacteria to be killed off.[‡] During this process the air in the jar will expand, increasing the pressure and 'burping' out through the loose rubber seal. Once the food is cooked, the seal is closed tight by screwing down the lid and the air inside begins to cool.

Cooling the air results in a drop in pressure inside the jar so external air pressure will serve to push the seal tighter and tighter. Once completely cold, the cooked, pasteurised food is stored in an airtight environment, sterilised by heat, and will last, unrefrigerated, for years.

In spite of incredible advances in home cooking, nothing has ever done the job of the preserving jar better, and it is one of the very few items in the modern kitchen that remains completely unchanged from its original incarnation.

---

[*] 1749–1841.

[†] See Can opener, page 63.

[‡] Raising food above a certain temperature and holding it there is 'pasteurisation'. The bacteria in milk, for example, are killed by heating to 63°C (145°F) for 30 minutes.

THE COOKING POT

REFERENCES TO 'DUTCH OVENS' crop up all over the English-speaking world. It's thought the expression originated when some of the earliest sand cast-iron kitchenware was exported from the Netherlands in the late 1600s. Beaten and riveted iron pots and cauldrons worked well over the coals, but a pot made of solid, homogenous cast iron, of regular thickness and a healthy weight, held and distributed heat better. Cooks of the time may not have understood the science, but they'd have got consistently better cooked, less burnt food out of a 'Dutch oven'.

Many cast-iron pots had a recess on the lid into which hot coals could be shovelled. This could generally increase the temperature or even brown the top of whatever was cooking inside. Once ovens were in common use, pots in the modern kitchen didn't need the additional hot coals on top and most pots or casseroles were designed with a domed top and with linings such as enamel that were easier to clean.

A decent heavy pot had several natural advantages aside from the conduction, distribution and storage of heat. The heavy lid sealed in the food, preserving flavour, steaming ingredients and even providing a modest 'pressure cooking' effect in some cases. Some pots were designed with the lid fitting into a U-shaped channel that could be filled with water to create a seal; others, particularly the more expensive status objects of later years, would have lid and base machined or ground to create near-airtight seals and flat bottoms for maximum contact with electric heating plates.

French cookware company Cousances (founded in 1553) gained a worldwide reputation for cast-iron cookware and in 1934 patented the 'Doufeu'. This was a heavy, enamelled Dutch oven, with a tight-machined seal and a depression in the lid that could be filled with ice. The principle was that the juices of the food, as it cooked, would condense on the lid and drip off cast protrusions, effectively self-basting. The Doufeu was designed to be used on top of the stove, over a low heat.

A popular development on the Doufeu was the British enamelled steel 'chicken roaster'. It was cheaper to manufacture and usually used inside the oven, but, nonetheless, used the same principle of condensation to self-baste.

In 1957 Cousance was bought by rivals 'Le Creuset'. Founded in 1925, Le Creuset had concentrated on enamelling and had introduced the unheard of and bewildering innovation of coloured finishes on cooking pots. The orange finish, supposedly inspired by the colour of molten iron, became a unique and effective trademark. Symbolic of the fashionable French provincial style of cooking, Le Creuset casseroles became the must-have item in home kitchens worldwide from the late 1960s onwards.

The 'Dutch Pot' (*opposite*) is a Jamaican descendant of the original Doufeu and an intrinsic part of the region's cuisine. Locally cast in aluminium rather than iron, it required seasoning if it was not to stick, and constant watching on a low flame. Even then it was prone to burning. The importance of a good seal, though, was fully understood, and it was not uncommon when buying a pot, to spend a long time trying

different base and lid combinations to achieve the best fit. Because a trusted, well-seasoned pot would be greatly valued, many of the Jamaican families moving to Britain from 1948 onwards brought their Dutch Pots with them.

There has always been something profoundly symbolic about the pot. The association with ancient food traditions, with family occasions and shared hospitality have meant that even in the most modern kitchen, earthenware and glazed china pots still hold a place of honour. The Scandinavian example, opposite, was probably made in the last few decades but its design is timeless. It can be used to cook and serve a very serviceable stew – as long as any browning of meat is done separately in a metal pan – but its value lies more in its visual effect. The brown glaze and the gently swelling maternal belly of its shape makes the pot just as significant a centrepiece to the family meal as a browned and spitting joint or a large stuffed bird.

A few kitchen objects reach the status of international design icons. Of these, this cast-iron cauldron is perhaps my favourite (*pictured on page 2*). Timo Sarpaneva was widely regarded as Finland's most important 20th-century industrial designer, creating works in glass, wood, metal and textiles that hang in galleries all over the world. But this deceptively simple iron pot is the piece that most seized the imagination, ending up on a Finnish postage stamp and in a glass case in probably every design museum in the world. Perhaps the best thing about it is that for all its clean lines and pared down, sculptural elegance, it feels like his most personal and emotional work.

Sarpaneva said he was influenced by the craftsmanship of his blacksmith grandfather, and that seems evident in the unashamed rough-cast finish of the pot's exterior. Compared to a traditional pot, the lines are simplified and straightened, but his main objective was to make something that could create a 'damn fine reindeer stew'. Like the Le Creuset, the pot is lined with enamel, which, though it does discolour a little with age and hard use, cannot take up the flavours of foods. It will also soak clean after even the most catastrophic burning. Like the Dutch Pot, the heavy lid is turned to fine tolerances and fits snugly into a lip, creating a semi 'pressure-cooking' effect that enhances long slow-simmering braises.

Perhaps the cleverest part of the pot is the wooden handle. This is inspired by the way you'd use a stick around a campfire, to lift the lid and stir. The tip of the handle can be inserted into the recess in the lid and used to open it. The handle is also intended to encourage the cook to carry the pot to the table for serving food. Other pots have evolved strong myths over centuries and are wreathed in traditions of use, but Sarpaneva took the myths and traditions and wove them back into his design.

I have to confess that my own Sarpaneva casserole is sometimes frustrating. It requires watching and gentle heat to avoid food 'catching' on the base, and at times I have used harsh words in its direction. But there is something so complete about the design, something in the way it plays back so many of the things we want to be true about a pot of stew, that I keep forgiving it and coming back to it. I have a suspicion that the way it's been designed means that the Sarpaneva may work best on a pot-bellied stove in a forest cabin and I'm not quite prepared to make that move…yet.

PRESTIGE KITCHEN TOOLS

IN HIS 1975 BOOK *The Cook's Catalogue* American food-writing legend James Beard railed at the quality of American spatulas. They were so poor, he said, that the cook should acquire an artist's palette knife instead.

It was perhaps a little obsessive of him to direct his ire at that particular utensil because most kitchen hand tools, being easy to mass-produce and with a vast and largely undiscriminating customer base, were not built with quality in mind.

Sets of kitchen tools were popular wedding gifts and there could be no greater reassurance for the young homemaker than to receive a similar set to the version one's parents had. For this reason the Prestige 'Skyline' range has remained the national standard in the UK for as long as any of us cares to remember. Though the colour scheme on the dipped wooden handles has changed to reflect fashion, the tools themselves are still an adequate grade of stainless steel, riveted together and pre-installed with comforting nostalgia.

The kit usually came with a hanging rack and could contain a whisk, a tomato slicer, a measuring, slotted or serving spoon and a carving fork. Other items were introduced and replaced over the decades, but the handle configuration and the odd 'school tie' colour schemes persisted.

The Skyline spatula, in particular, is a neglected design classic: pared down, austere and ineluctably 'Festival of Britain'. A flexible blade, pierced with long slots terminates in a flat, sharp edge, purpose-built for scraping carbonised crispy pancakes off a peeling 'non-stick' pan. The broad surface enables the cook to lift overcooked plaice into packet parsley sauce without the fish falling apart and, for those special romantic evenings in, the highly chromed surface will withstand flaming with Cointreau while rolling crêpes.

It's not just a tool, it's a fetish: a single object containing the whole of your family's culinary history from your mum's first fried egg to your most recent dinner party triumph. Skyline tools might not be the most perfectly functional design nor, indeed, the most aesthetically pleasing, but they have a place in all our hearts that can never be supplanted by novelty. I respect James Beard as an expert in our field, but he only had to buy an artist's palette knife because he didn't have a Skyline spatula.

DEEP-FAT FRYER (CHIP PAN)

TO FRY FOOD COMPLETELY immersed in boiling fat is as dangerous as it is delicious. Written recipes going back as far as the Romans suggest it as a technique, usually using olive oil, which will give a reasonable result at comparatively low temperatures. In Chinese and Japanese cooking, sesame, nut oils or animal fats – which can cook hotter – were used, but in a wok or wide pan and often outdoors. Because the food is kept moving in a wok, it's a slightly different kind of frying.*

When the British think of fried food, though, they think of chips and that means something else. The Ideal Chip, the sort we grew to love in chip shops,† was fried in big deep tanks of dripping at around 185°C (365°F). When dropped in, the potatoes gave off steam that boiled off and the resulting chip would, if the customer was lucky, remain dry and crisp.

When the British started cooking chips in home kitchens, the results were little short of a national disaster. The chip pan was originally a pot roughly as deep as it was wide, about two-thirds filled with oil or dripping and sometimes equipped with a basket to hold food. In many households, thrifty cooks would add waste or recovered drippings or other fats to the chip pan, resulting in a complex and muddled flavour developing over time. At 185°C, dripping, or even vegetable oil, is as flammable as diesel. If it boiled over the top of an overfilled pan when the chips were dropped in, it would catch on the gas flame and shoot a burst of searing flame straight to the kitchen ceiling. If the cook tried to douse the flames with water, the boiling oil would erupt, spraying everything in the room with flame and accelerant. It is only in very recent years that 'chip pan fires' have ceased to be the biggest source of house fires in UK fire brigade statistics.

A domestic deep-fat fryer with a thermostatically controlled electric element and safety features like a maximum-fill line and an airtight lid answer many of the dangers of deep frying. However, these devices have grown to popularity at almost precisely the time that consumers are discovering the health threats of eating too much fat. In the UK, ownership of a deep-fat fryer is laden with problems. We love chips and we want to cook them at home, but we remember the fryer as lethal and increasingly believe the chips themselves will kill us. As in everything British there are issues of class inherent in the idea of eating chips at all, and now the problem of dealing with waste oil has made us aware of the environmental impact of domestic deep frying. We could probably make a confident prediction that the deep-fat fryer will no longer have a place in the home kitchen in a decade, and that deep-fried food will only be purchased from professional vendors as an occasional treat, as it originally was.

---

* Somewhere between Western deep and shallow frying.

† Chips first became popular as a mass-produced street food in France in the 1830s, where they were cooked outdoors in large tanks of horse fat.

KETTLE

THE KETTLE IS A PROFOUNDLY domestic appliance, existing only where there is a culture of tea. Coffee can be made in a jug, pot or pan because, in most cases, the coffee is heated while it brews. Tea requires that water be boiled first, carried to a separate pot and poured over the leaves.

A kettle is closed, apart from the spout, and so heating is more efficient than in an open vessel. Kettles worked on open fires, in domestic fireplaces and on kitchen ranges. Some were even adapted so the pressure of steam would activate a whistle, preventing the kettle from 'boiling dry'. The first electric kettles appeared in the 1890s and are attributed to the UK company Compton and Co. Nobody at this early stage was quite confident enough to mix water and electricity in a domestic setting and so the Compton model was a copper and brass kettle with an electric heating coil outside and underneath, protected by a metal ring.

The problem was eventually solved by Birmingham engineers Bulpitt and Sons in 1922, when they developed a heating coil sealed inside a metal tube that could be immersed in the water. They sold the kettle under the brand name Swan. These early models could still boil dry: when all the water in an unattended kettle had boiled away, there would be nothing to conduct the heat away from the element, which would continue to run, uncontrolled. Kettle elements were some of the highest-drawing electrical appliances in the home and, without control, it was not unusual for the element, casing or kettle to melt or to set the counter on fire. One early safety device was a plug and socket containing a brass rod on the back of the kettle. If the kettle got dangerously hot, the rod would expand, pushing out the plug and severing the connection to the mains.

In 1955 the Russell Hobbs company introduced the 'K1' kettle, which featured a bimetallic strip thermostat to switch off the power the moment the water boiled; there have been few true innovations since. The kettle remains a peculiarly important part of British domestic culture, to such an extent that 'put the kettle on, love' is as valid a greeting to one's partner on arriving home as 'good evening, darling'.

SOUS-VIDE

THE PRINCIPLE OF SOUS-VIDE cooking is simple. There is a temperature at which food is considered 'done' and in conventional cooking the surface of the food is raised to way above this point so that the core is perfectly cooked. This is why bread and cake and steak will all have delicious caramelised 'crusts' on them when their centres are perfectly finished. In sous-vide cooking the food is sealed in a pouch and held in an environment at precisely the 'done' temperature. If a steak is medium rare at a core temperature of 56.6°C (134°F) then it is cooked by holding it in a water bath of exactly that temperature until it is evenly hot throughout. This usually takes longer than conventional cooking, but the advantage is that you can't overcook. Even if you leave the food in the tank overnight it stays perfect.

The system was first used in professional kitchens in France in 1974 when Georges Pralus used it to poach foie gras at the La Maison Troisgros. It has since been taken up with alacrity by chefs all over the world.

Because the food can be prepared, stored and frozen in the pouch and cooking can be so precisely controlled, it is also the ideal system for institutional cooking and in places where food safety is a concern. Even more than in Michelin-starred restaurants, sous-vide has become the preferred way to serve prepared meals in pubs, schools, hospitals and on aircraft. It is untouched by human hands – until it is tipped on to the plate.

Whether you regard the sous-vide machine as a convenient home tool or a stupendously complicated piece of restaurant gadgetry seems to depend entirely on which country you live in. Home users in some places love the convenience of being able to pull a pouch out of the freezer, drop it in the tank, set the timer before leaving for work and returning to a perfectly cooked meal. For them it's just a high-tech improvement on the Crock-Pot (see page 128). In the UK and the US, sous-vide equipment seems to have stayed in the professional kitchen where chefs assiduously challenge the boundaries of time and temperature in the constant search for novel tastes and textures.

Manufacturers of prepared food are excited about the prospects of sous-vide for future use in home food 'systems'. Ready meals ordered online and then home cooked in a proprietary sous-vide appliance would be a perfect closed loop of profitability. Although manufacturers are not printing sous-vide cooking instructions on the packets yet, many domestic versions of the equipment are already wirelessly connectable. At the moment, the machine can be controlled remotely via a smartphone app, but would, in time, be equally capable of downloading its own cooking instructions from the web or reading them from an RFID label on the packaging.

SERVING

WOODEN SALAD BOWL AND TOSSERS

THE WOODEN SALAD BOWL with matching wooden tossers – preferably purchased while on holiday in Provence and never, ever washed – is a ritual object in the well-equipped home kitchen. Restaurants and other commercial establishments have naturally avoided using a communal serving vessel that can't be properly cleaned between uses. How on earth did such an odd tradition arise?

It's often assumed that the bowl 'takes on' flavours over time – particularly that of garlic which, some cooks recommend, can be rubbed raw into the bowl. Depending on where the writer stands on garlic, this is either to produce a massively strong garlic flavour or, in another explanation, to impart a more subtle flavour than raw garlic might in the dressing itself. Elizabeth David, when asked to pass judgement on the idea is said to have responded waspishly that it depended whether you were intending to eat the bowl or the salad. In a way this is an unsurprising response. David was never keen on American innovations in the kitchen and it transpires that the wooden salad bowl was exactly that.

In 1936 American food writer George Rector began championing the wooden bowl in his popular columns in the *Saturday Evening Post*. He claimed to have picked up the idea from a French chef called Hippolyte Arnion and describes an al fresco meal where he believed the bowl 'flavoured' his crisp green salad. From that point onwards Rector seemed almost obsessed with his discovery, making it his trademark gimmick,* and he repeatedly reinforced the idea that '… after you've been rubbing your bowl with garlic and anointing it with oil for some years, it will have acquired the patina of a Corinthian bronze and the personality of a 100-year-old brandy'.† Soon the 'never-washed' wooden salad bowl began to crop up in kitchens across America. It has been suggested that as 'dressing the salad' was often the job of the father of the household and featured his own 'special recipe', the mystery and theatre of the unwashed bowl fitted naturally into the tableside drama.

The wooden salad bowl eventually became so completely symbolic of kitchen aspirations that Sir Terence Conran's approach to democratising design was described thus: 'The problem with Terence is that he wants the whole world to have a better salad bowl.'

---

* Rector, to his credit, was also an enthusiastic advocate for freshly ground black pepper and was responsible for popularising grinders in the US.

† The only persistent flavour that writers since Rector have identified in a 'patinated' bowl is rancid salad oil.

BISCUIT TIN

THE WORD 'BISCUIT' derives from the Latin *bis coctus* ('cooked twice'). At its simplest the biscuit is a piece of cake or bread that has been baked a second time to drive off any remaining moisture. Dried in this way, the biscuit will remain edible for as long as it is kept in a dry, airtight container. Biscuits' long shelf life meant that they were commonly used as rations for travellers, sailors and soldiers, supplying nourishment where there were no cooking facilities and in houses where regular baking was not possible.

In working-class Victorian homes, biscuits were an important part of the family diet and, as they could be cheaply mass produced, they became some of the first products to be branded. Manufacturers* created and promoted particular shapes and flavours that became favourites, and a tin of biscuits, offering sweetness and perhaps an element of choice in an otherwise unvarying diet, soon became regarded as an affordable luxury – particularly in the UK where biscuits' association with tea made them something akin to a national dish.

Manufacturers supplied tins that kept biscuits in good condition, and were cheap to produce and print with brands and advertising messages. Wealthier homes would have a purpose-made, unbranded 'biscuit barrel', but for many working-class families the tin was useful, attractive and functional.

Biscuit tins survived far beyond their original purpose and remain in many of our kitchens to this day, hidden, often neglected, containing spare screws, old batteries, first-aid supplies, plant seeds, string and, very occasionally, biscuits.

---

* The brand names of biscuits and their manufacturers are so loved in the UK that you can
   generate Betjemanesque poetry or Alan Bennett-style reminiscences simply by listing them:

   Peek Freans, Garibaldi.
   Huntley & Palmers, Viscount.
   Jacob's, Carr's, MacFarlane Lang.
   McVities, Crawford's, Custard Cream.

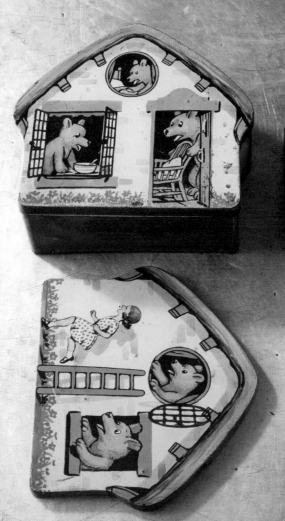

JELLY MOULDS

THE HISTORY OF GELATINE in food is long and varied. Dishes using gelatine extracted from animal bones and hooves go back almost as long as we have recorded recipes. Eliza Acton and Hannah Glasse both recommend gelatines as easily digestible and nourishing for invalids, and aspic-coated foods were some of the most elaborate presentations on aristocratic tables. The copper moulds we see in illustrations of palace kitchens were, occasionally, used for gelatines, but were more likely to be used in a dozen other kinds of moulded preparations. Anything from ice cream to mashed potato could be presented moulded, but the key point was that the production of a gelatine clear enough for elegant food use was hard work and involved both staff and space.

In 1897 in LeRoy, New York, a patent medicine manufacturer called Pearle Wait spotted an opportunity in the powdered gelatines that were beginning to be mass produced to industrial scale. By adding colouring and flavouring powders, he cut out all the complex kitchen processes and created an 'instant' colourful dessert that he named 'Jell-O'. Jell-O was marketed directly and cleverly to householders. Moving from town to town, salesmen in uniform and driving matched gigs would deliver Jell-O recipe leaflets to every house in town before approaching the local grocer to stock the dessert.

Jelly was in many ways the perfect product for modern marketing. The raw material is effectively a refined waste product of the industrial meat industry, but Wait's brilliant insight turned it into something bright, tasty, simple, clean and modern that appealed to parents, children, cooks and householders. 'Jelly' took off with equal success in other countries around the world.

In spite of its instant convenience, brightly coloured, cheap, versatile jelly encouraged simple creativity in the home kitchen. A bowl of jelly pleases children, but a shape set in a simple glass mould creates the sort of centrepiece that delights the assembled crowd and turns a family meal into a memorable feast.

Though some glass moulds recall the original architectural shapes of Victorian copper moulds, it was the rabbit-shaped version that somehow most grabbed kids' imaginations. Copper 'rabbit' moulds were originally used to present terrines and pâtés in a slightly macabre zoomorphism, but found a new life made of glass or plastic moulds for children's desserts.

BREAD BIN

BREAD IS A COMPLEX THING to store. Fresh bread is moist and possibly warm. If it's left out on the counter it will dry out and 'stale'; if it's wrapped tightly enough not to dry, it grows mould very quickly. The bread 'bin'* is a reasonable compromise solution to the storage problem – but that's only half the story.

The final stages of traditional breadmaking, before cooking, are all about shaping. It's probably the most complex and skilled part of the baker's art. For the bread to stay light and airy, the dough must be wet and floppy and it is held in shape while cooking by careful manipulation of the surface layer of the ball of dough. The tough, elastic layer where dough meets air is what bakes to form the 'crust' and in skilled hands the dough can be shaped into a ball, stick or oval shape that will 'stand up' on the oven floor.

In the mid-19th century as urban populations grew, bread became the vital staple and began to be produced on an industrial scale. Shaping, the traditional craft skill, was time-consuming and expert bakers were expensive, and so the tin loaf evolved. In the UK and almost immediately in the US and Australia, the standard loaf became the brick shape we now recognise.

Urban families had no facility for home baking and so bought loaves that had to be cut for serving† and then stored for as long as necessary.

The French 'baguette' is standardised by government decree. There is a lovely myth that the shape evolved so that Napoleon's soldiers could better fit the loaves into their backpacks or even down their trouser legs, but in fact, the baguette is relatively simple to hand-shape, has a much smaller cut surface once you've started eating it and is a smaller size – not really intended to be stored. A baguette lasts a day – quite literally 'daily bread' – and, as a result the nation that gave birth to Brillat-Savarin is a stranger to the bread bin.

---

* Usually called a breadbox in the US.

† Once sliced into, a loaf loses even the limited preservative protection of the crust and will go stale much faster.

TEA TOWEL

THERE HAVE BEEN learned works written about printed T-shirts. Cheap to buy, easy to produce and, after a short period of proud public display, effectively disposable, T-shirts have legitimately been interpreted as a kind of folk art. But the T-shirt too often represents a shallow and short-lived loyalty. For me the tea towel is the more meaningful medium.

We have probably used cloths in cooking for as long as we've cooked. They're great for mopping up spills and, even when there's nothing purpose-made around, a cook will improvise with apron or clothing to pick up something hot without getting burned. It can't have taken cooks long to realise that linen was a particularly effective material in the kitchen, both for its qualities of absorption and the hard surface of its fibres which create a superior polish on silver, china or glass.

Flax had been woven into fabrics in ancient Egypt* and it's been suggested that Phoenician traders were the first to bring the plant to Ireland. In fact, it was a fleeing Huguenot, Louis Crommelin, who brought the techniques of linen production to Belfast in the 1690s. By 1870 Belfast and the surrounding towns were producing the majority of the world's linen cloth, including the first pieces intentionally made and marketed as kitchen cloths – or the more refined 'tea towel'† ('dish towel' in the US).

Early towels had a simple strip of dyed threads woven in to identify the manufacturer, but it wasn't long before companies began printing tea towels to order.

I still experience an immense surge of nostalgia when I see a tea towel from the seaside town where I grew up or the county in which I was born. It's not simply the old image, but more that tea towels were so often a way of expressing a wonderful, now lost, civic pride.

In the UK, the mass production of tea towels is almost the defining characteristic of a significant national event. Beautiful examples from the Festival of Britain still change hands for large sums, though the millions of wonky knock-offs sold to celebrate the wedding of Prince Charles to Lady Diana Spencer will probably never realise the sums their owners hoped for.

Perhaps because they were cheap to produce, useful and instantly expressive, tea towels were a perfect souvenir, an ideal gift. Looking at them with modern eyes, there is something incredibly moving about wanting to remember a trip to Lincolnshire, about the sense of wonder inspired by a dam and irrigation project (see photographs on pages 160–1). In the 'three-colour' process‡ the pigments combine to

---

* Linen was used both to stuff and to wrap the bodies of dead pharaohs.

† During the tea-drinking craze of the 18th century the pot and 'dishes', too delicate to be entrusted to the kitchen staff for cleaning, were washed and dried by the lady of the house.

‡ This book is printed in four colours, the three 'process' inks that combine to make any colour and a fourth black plate that delivers the text with maximum intensity.

produce a full range of natural colours in an image, but most tea towels have been screen printed, a technique in which the colours remain separate. The image is built up from blocks of colour, laid on to the fabric in consecutive passes. This is the same idiosyncratic effect that we've grown to love in comic books and can, say, in the hands of an artist like Andy Warhol, produce amazing results. From a design point of view we can but admire the artist who felt equal to expressing the wide, wild beauty, the stunning natural diversity of the entire continent of Australia in black, green, yellow, red, two tones of blue and half a square metre of linen.

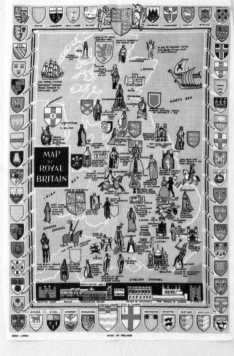

ENERGY CONSUMPTION

UNIT OF MEASUREMENT – ONE KILOWATT HOUR (KWH) EQUAL TO 1,000
WATT HOURS (OR THE CONSUMPTION OF A 1KW FIRE FOR 1 HOUR).

SMOOTHING IRON	SPIN DRYER	DISH WASHER	IMMERSION HEATER	REFRIGERATOR	TUMBLER DRYER
OVER 2 HOURS FOR 1 UNIT.	5 WEEKS LAUNDRY FOR 1 UNIT.	A FAMILY'S DINNER DISHES FOR ABOUT 1 UNIT.	3 KW – 3 UNITS PER HOUR.	POPULAR SIZE ABOUT 1 UNIT PER DAY.	1 HOUR FOR 1 UNIT.
FREEZER CHEST	FREEZER UPRIGHT	COOKER	HEATERS	WASHING MACHINE	WASHING MACHINE
1½–1¾ UNITS PER CU. FT. PER WEEK.	1½–2 UNITS PER CU. FT. PER WEEK.	4 UNITS A DAY FOR FAMILY OF 4	FAN OR RADIANT 2 KW – 2 UNITS PER HOUR	TWIN TUB: WEEKLY WASH FOR FAMILY OF 4 – 3 UNITS	AUTOMATIC: WEEKLY WASH FOR FAMILY OF 4

FOR 1 UNIT OF ELECTRICITY YOU CAN USE

BATTERY CHARGER	BLANKET	BLENDER	CAN OPENER	CARVING KNIFE	COFFEE PERCOLATOR
FOR 50 HOURS	OVER: ALL NIGHT FOR 1/3 MONTHS. UNDER: EVERY NIGHT FOR A WEEK	TO MAKE 500 PTS. OF SOUP	TO OPEN ABOUT 6,250 CANS.	TO CARVE 220 WEEKEND JOINTS	TO MAKE ABOUT 75 CUPS
CLOCK	EXTRACTOR	FLOOR POLISHER	HAIR DRYER	HAIR ROLLERS	FOOD MIXER
FOR 3 MONTHS	FOR 24 HOURS.	FOR 2½ HRS.	FOR 3 HRS.	FOR 22 TREATMENTS.	TO MIX 67 CAKES.
KETTLE	LIGHT	POWER DRILL	RADIO	RAZOR	SEWING MACHINE
TO BOIL ABOUT 12 PINTS	100W. LAMP GIVES YOU FLUORESCENT FOR OVER: TUBE GIVES 4 TIMES LIGHT OF 100W LAMP	FOR 4 HOURS DRILLING	FOR 30 HOURS	FOR 1,800 SHAVES	TO SEW ELEVEN CHILDREN'S DRESSES
TELEVISION	TAPE RECORDER	TOASTER	VACUUM CLEANER	RECORD PLAYER	WASTE DISPOSAL
COLOUR: 3 HRS. B/W: 7 HRS.	FOR 24 HOURS.	TO MAKE 70 SLICES OF TOAST.	FOR 2 HOURS.	FOR 24 HOURS.	TO GRIND 1 CWT. RUBBISH.

Blackstaff

TEAPOT

THE TEAPOT HAD A LONG and distinguished life in other parts of the home before it arrived in the kitchen. When tea first became fashionable in England in the 17th century it was the object of the aristocracy and, more particularly, the women of the household. The teapot was a beautiful piece of silver or ceramic, perhaps kept in a fitted, velvet-lined case. It would be kept under lock and key in the room where the lady of the house served tea to her guests, along with a locked tea caddy for the precious leaves. Servants might bring hot water from the kitchens or a kettle with a spirit lamp could be provided for the truly independent brewer, but the teapot itself was a potent status symbol and accorded a suitable place of honour.

With the advent of tea production and imports on a massive scale from across the Empire, the habit of drinking it soon moved down through the social classes and, by the latter part of the 18th century, as the working classes began moving to cities in pursuit of work, tea was firmly part of the staple diet for even the poorest. A kettle would sing on the fire and the teapot, kept easily accessible on a table or sideboard, could be kept constantly charged. In the poorest housing, with no separate kitchen in any recognisable sense, the teapot and kettle, close to the hearth, were symbolic of the heart of the home.

When purpose-built kitchens began appearing in new housing, with sources of heat and water easily to hand, it was natural for tea-making to move there. Today the teapot lives firmly on the kitchen counter and tea is drunk informally in mugs rather than in teacups and saucers. It's pleasing, though, that we still retain as a ritual of hospitality the ability to 'make a pot' and carry it into another room of the house when important guests visit.

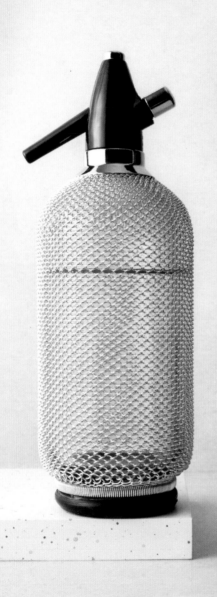

SODA SYPHON & SODASTREAM

ONE OF THE EARLIEST references to a device for carbonating water at home is to the Gasogene in Sherlock Holmes.* This comprised two joined glass spheres with a tap on the top, bound in a tight wicker cage that prevented explosions. The lower vessel was filled with water, the top with a mixture of tartaric acid and bicarbonate of soda, which reacted to give off carbon dioxide. In the enclosed space, the gas was forced into the water, 'carbonating' it and creating 'soda water.' For centuries, naturally carbonated mineral waters had been bottled at source and sold as a luxury, but the Gasogene brought the technology for making one's own right into the household.

Soda 'syphons' were pre-pressurised bottles of soda water with a tap at the top for serving. Once filled and pressurised at the factory, they could be stored satisfactorily for a long time before being delivered to customers. Suppliers would pick up the empties and return them for refilling. This explains why many of the lovely syphons in pictures of cocktail drinking in the 1920s came with a protective wire cage. As long as they didn't get smashed in transit these syphons were the ultimate recyclable.

Since the 1890s British company Aerators Limited had been producing metal 'bulbs' of pressurised CO_2 that could be used in their own rechargeable syphons. These became affordable, safe and common in the home in 1945, when the company, now renamed Sparklets, ceased wartime production of small-arms ammunition and launched the metal 'Streamline' syphon.

In 1955 the SodaStream was introduced in the UK, equipped with an exchangeable CO_2 reservoir that could aerate up to 60 litres of water. It was soon available in Australia, New Zealand and eventually in the US but, unlike other kitchen appliances, the SodaStream machine alone was useless without a national supply network for gas and syrups. The SodaStream was heavily advertised to young people, who were enjoined with infectious jingles to 'Get busy with the fizzy' – advertising campaigns that are even today regarded as case studies in 'pester power'. Many people remember the SodaStream with great fondness, perhaps because it really felt like the first piece of cool technology that was made with our childhood desires in mind.

Key to the SodaStream's appeal was the range of flavouring syrups, which the company cleverly supplied via licensing arrangements with already successful drinks brands. Kids were delighted to 'make their own' Pepsi, Tizer or Fanta. Meanwhile, the company boss referred to a 'razor blade' business model in which the machine itself is just the starting point of a lifetime of purchasing gas cylinders and syrups.

We're already used to buying filters for our water jugs and 'pods' for our coffee machines, but there's no reason to think we might not end up with whole meals being delivered in a form that fits a single proprietary cooking device.

---

* *A Scandal in Bohemia.* Holmes tosses Dr Watson a box of cigars and points him towards 'a spirit case and gasogene in the corner'.

FONDUE SET

PERHAPS IT'S ENGLISH uptightness, but to me there is something profoundly silly about fondue. For my generation, which just missed the fondue boom, it will forever be tinged with what it was used to represent in films and print ads. Fondue was shared food, so it was always featured in shots that hinted at seduction, or worse, the sort of glamorous 'international' dinner parties that teetered on the edge of swinging. The ever-so-slightly-forced intimacy of the shared pot of melted cheese was a useful symbol, but fell irretrievably into the same smutty comic category as the phallic pepper grinder* and games of Twister.

This is partly unfair. There had long been a tradition of eating melted cheese as a dip in many parts of the world and it was not uncommon in the Swiss lowlands near the French border. It is here that the darker story of fondue begins to bubble ...

Originally formed in 1914, the Schweizer Käseunion AG was a trade body and cartel that controlled the production of Swiss cheeses and promoted their sale worldwide. Having remained neutral through the First World War, Switzerland found itself with more surplus cheese than it could sell to the rest of Europe – much of which still maintained tariffs and trade restrictions. In the 1930s the Käseunion campaigned to have fondue acknowledged as the Swiss national dish and published a series of regional-variant recipes, partly as what they described as a 'spiritual defence' of Swiss nationality – and partly because fondue used such a colossal amount of cheese.

In spite of military neutrality, the Käseunion had created a WMD for cultural warfare and after the end of the Second World War and subsequent rationing, they deployed it globally. At the 1964 World's Fair in New York fondue was served at the Swiss Pavilion. It was accompanied by an advertising campaign featuring attractive, hearty young Swiss, partying around the steaming bowl, and kick-started an immediate and resounding craze.† In Britain, meanwhile, with package holidays gaining in popularity, the fondue set became something of a status symbol among those who wanted their guests to know they went skiing.

The fondue pot is more correctly called a caquelon and was traditionally made of earthenware. Later versions were made of cast iron, which, though attractive, is a better conductor of heat, meaning that the fondue would often catch and stick to the bottom. 'Tradition' holds that this crust, also know as *la religieuse* (or 'the nun') is a delicacy.‡ Although, in the bizarre and questionable back-story of the fondue, that might just be another terrific piece of propaganda from the Cheese Union.

---

* See page 14.

† The Schweizer Käseunion AG folded in 1999 in a corruption scandal.

‡ Other 'traditions' suggest that dropping your bread in the fondue is 'bad luck' which can only be repaired by buying a round of drinks if you are male or kissing all the other diners if female.

ON
THE KITCHEN
ENVIRONMENT

I T'S NOT JUST THE utensils and appliances that have improved life in the modern kitchen. If we examine our own kitchens today, the most influential advances are often effectively invisible. It's the materials, the structure, indeed, the whole environment that has changed the most.

It was either Samuel Bentham[*] or Immanuel Nobel[†] who first came up with the idea of laminating veneers of timber to make strong, thin, light and dimensionally stable board. They both invented lathes that created veneers in industrial quantities and can lay equal claim to the accolade 'Father of Plywood'. Much of the earliest kitchen cabinetry was made of this innovative material that also had the advantage of being cheap. As kitchen cupboards were usually painted or enamelled for reasons of hygiene, it didn't matter that the wood lacked a visually pleasing grained surface. Plywood furniture was light, cheap to make and hard-wearing enough to survive a long working life.

Modernist designers and architects were inspired by high-tech new materials and Charles and Ray Eames, Arne Jacobsen, Wells Coates and Walter Gropius all made extensive use of plywood. The Frankfurt Kitchen, of course, was predominantly plywood.

Particle board was invented in Germany in 1932 by Max Himmelheber[‡]. The original 'recycled' material, it was made by compressing a mixture of workshop sawdust and chippings into boards with a combination of phenolic resin and high pressure. Particle board had very little structural strength, but was amazingly cheap to produce and when, after the Second World War, companies began looking for cost-effective ways to make furniture, particle board fitted the brief. It was hopeless in the presence of water – it 'blew up' and then disintegrated – but, when bound in the new

---

* 1757–1831, brother of the more famous Jeremy Bentham, philosopher.

† 1801–72, father of the more famous Alfred Nobel, inventor of dynamite.

‡ Himmelheber served in the Luftwaffe during the Second World War, was shot down over Kent in 1940 and spent the rest of the war as a POW in Woolwich.

Formica laminate (see below), it had a reasonable life expectancy at low cost. Most of the early kit-kitchen systems were made with Formica-bound particle board.

Medium density fibreboard (MDF) was developed in the 1980s and uses ground wood dust bound with glue to create a tough, grainless composite that's easy to work and has a longer life than particle board. The IKEA company, the largest manufacturer of furniture in the world* at the time of writing, harvests trees that are turned straight into MDF, which is easier to machine accurately than natural timber. This quality is significant as almost all the work is now done by computer-controlled cutting equipment (CNC) and robots.

Justus von Liebig should, if there were any justice in the world, be regarded as the patron saint of the kitchen. The insanely prolific German chemist is famous for his invention of the beef extract that became OXO and the yeast concentration process that gave the world Marmite, but it's less well known that he was also the first person to synthesise melamine.

Melamine is a compound with uses in agriculture, pharmaceuticals and other industries, but is most interesting (from a culinary perspective) when mixed with formaldehyde to create a thermoplastic resin.† Tough, resilient, mouldable, inert in the presence of foodstuffs or most chemicals, melamine resin was quickly brought into the kitchen in the form of early 'plastic' vessels and utensils.

In 1913 two scientists, Daniel J. O'Conor and Herbert A. Faber, while working at Westinghouse, came up with the idea of soaking layers of absorbent 'brown' paper in phenolic resin and

---

* IKEA is responsible for one per cent of the world's consumption of timber.

† We sometimes hear of melamine in cases of food adulteration and people are often baffled as to why such a substance should be added to food. Pure melamine, when added to food, makes it perform better in tests of protein content, so unscrupulous manufacturers of baby formula and animal feed have sometimes used it to boost their prices. As melamine is toxic to humans even in small concentrations, this scam misfired with catastrophic results.

then baking it under pressure. Initially they thought of it as a substitute for an existing electrical insulator – a substitute 'for mica' – and in February 1913 they filed the first patent for Formica.

At first Formica was sold as a solid, machineable material for engineering use – it was used to make cogs and gears that went into 'silent' Chevrolet gearboxes – but in 1938 Westinghouse began making Formica with melamine. Because melamine set clear, it allowed patterns printed on the layers of paper to show through.

Formica was immediately seen as a wonder material by kitchen designers. Used as a veneer, it protected cheap wood composites, was hygienic and hard-wearing, and offered almost unlimited potential for colour and imagery. As the dull years of post-war austerity and furniture rationing (see page 45) drew to a close, customers were looking for bright, exciting new options.

Other companies patented similar laminate products to compete with Formica but it managed to remain brand leader. It was the combination of a hard-wearing covering over economical composite materials that made kit-form fitted kitchens like Hygena QA possible… and most importantly, affordable. It's arguable that Formica is the single advance in materials science that has done the most to further the development of the domestic kitchen.

In later years the ubiquity of Formica meant that there was a small market for more premium worktops. For a while, custom-cut marble and granite came back into fashion amongst the wealthy and, more recently, high-tech cast plastic systems like Corian have become the fashionable choice for those who would never stoop to a 'Formica kitchen'.

For those afforded the luxury of planning and building a kitchen from scratch the ideal flooring material would be stone or tile. It's entirely waterproof, easy to keep clean and resistant to bugs and pests, but as smaller family dwellings began to be built, at speed, in the new industrial cities, there was little time or inclination for such expensive luxuries. On a regular timber floor a covering material becomes an important factor in comfort and hygiene.

The earliest kitchen floor coverings were 'oilcloths' made from canvas stretched on a frame and painted with thin layers of boiled linseed oil.* Linseed is a 'drying' oil which means that, over time, it polymerises into a solid. This made it a suitable base for paint, both on the exterior woodwork of houses and the 'oil' paintings that hung on the walls inside.†

Oilcloth could be bought off a roll at a hardware store or chandlers, but the resourceful householder could stretch out cloth on an outside wall and paint it with cheap linseed-based paint for a similar effect.

'Linoleum'‡ was invented in 1855 by Frederick Walton.§ He managed to speed up the time that linseed oil took to polymerise by boiling it with metal salts, and mixed the resulting mixture with powdered cork to create a thick, tough coating that was applied to a canvas base.

'Lino' was pretty exciting stuff.¶ It could be dyed and printed with patterns which, though hardly psychedelic by modern standards, were positively invigorating in the dark brown world of Victorian decoration. The cork powder made the material just a little more yielding than bare floor – which made standing for hours a little less painful and meant that a few of the pieces of china inevitably dropped, didn't actually smash.

Because it could be sterilised with hot water and was resistant to soaps and bleaches, linoleum became the standard flooring in hospitals and other institutions – the sort of rigorous fitness of

---

* Linseed oil is extracted from flax seed.

† It was also combined with chalk to make glazer's putty, used as a varnish on wood and as a penetrating dressing on cricket bats.

‡ From the Latin *linum* meaning 'flax' and *oleum* meaning 'oil'.

§ Linoleum may well be one of the most important cultural exports of Staines in Middlesex – Walton opened a factory there in 1864.

¶ Cordelia: So does looking at guns really make girls wanna have sex? That's scary.
Xander: Yeah, I guess.
Cordelia: Well, does looking at guns make *you* wanna have sex?
Xander: I'm seventeen. Looking at *linoleum* makes me wanna have sex.
From *Buffy the Vampire Slayer*, 'Innocence' (season 2, episode 14).

purpose that delighted the Modernists who would, by the look of some of their designs, have coated the walls with the wonder product if they thought they could have got away with it.

It's difficult to comprehend today the importance that used to be attached to a clean floor. In grand houses, the shine of a high polish was symbolic of the unlimited person-power at the owner's command. Like other status goods – silver, glass, exotic wood furniture – it wasn't just that you could afford the object but that you could afford its constant upkeep. On ships, in prisons, and military buildings, decks and floors were kept constantly polished by crew or inmates – painful and inherently futile labour which, though often explained as part of 'discipline', was essentially an expression of institutional power over the individual.

What is surprising is how powerful this symbol remained in the homes of ordinary workers. There are many contemporary descriptions of housewives spending hours on their knees, scrubbing tiles or stone with a hard brush. Well into the 1970s, in the North of England particularly, the 'good' houses in a working-class terrace could be distinguished by a step polished and whitened daily and an area of the pavement outside scrubbed clean. Given the amount of heavy physical labour in a house without washing machines or hoovers, one would have expected symbolic floor cleanliness to be sacrificed but, though Lino could be easily brushed, mopped and would look spankingly new in minutes, it was soon discovered that lino could be polished to a shine with beeswax – a rather ironic reversal for something so fundamentally labour-saving.

In the 1970s lino was largely superseded by 'vinyl' flooring. This was almost as hard-wearing but cheaper and more colourful than lino, fitting in with the bright 'pop' designs of the period and more appropriate to the budgets of struggling young homemakers. Vinyl flooring, if you believed the ads for cleaning products, could be made to gleam merely by a glamorous young woman in a circular skirt pirouetting over it, brandishing a light mop like a cheerleader for healthy, efficient modernity.

A working kitchen is a busy space. Incoming ingredients have to be washed, waste is generated, there are unpleasant smells. Cooking, by its nature, involves heat, but also exhaust gases from combustion along with steam and smoke. It is no coincidence that the more stately the home, the further the architect would have placed the kitchen from the living space of the owners. In the southern states of the USA and the homes of the Raj in India, kitchens were sited in separate buildings, as far from the house as possible – partly to minimise the risk of fire, but probably just as much to keep the kitchen servants and their unpleasant tasks out of sight and smell.

The atmosphere of the kitchen though, could be more than merely unpleasant; it could be lethal. The renowned French chef Antonin Carême died in 1833 of what is now believed to have been chronic carbon monoxide poisoning and anthracosis, brought on by years of cooking over charcoal. We can only assume that thousands of professional cooks all over the world, lacking Carême's celebrity, must have suffered a similar fate, unacknowledged.

When Alexis Soyer designed the kitchens for the Brighton Pavilion in the 19th century, he ensured that the room was of vast, soaring height so noxious fumes could move upwards, above the heads of the working chefs, and be expelled through vents cleverly concealed in columns painted to resemble palm trees.

In home kitchens the problem of ventilation was much worse. Mayhew, Orwell, Dickens and countless other social commentators mention the smells of working-class homes, particularly the pervasive odours of cheap food – fried bacon or boiled cabbage. To these largely middle-class observers, fed at home by servants from a discrete kitchen, this smell was the most alien part of their experience.

In many urban multiple-occupancy homes, tenants kept some of the cooking smells away from their living space by locating the gas ring or cooker in the common areas. Well-designed homes would place the cooking area next to a window or back door, and perforated 'air bricks' or grilles, placed high up on an outside wall, allowed fumes and smells to escape. Electric fans, as they became available, could be used to increase the airflow through the kitchen.[*]

---

[*] According to their company history, the Ventaxia company were asked by Winston Churchill to install extractor fans in 10 Downing St in 1945.

A commercial kitchen today can't run without a complicated extraction system that not only cools the working area but filters out polluting materials from the exhaust air, plus it needs to be fully wired in to fire control and gas supply systems. In the home the extractor hood has become ubiquitous, influencing, yet again, the way in which we design our kitchens. Having, for generations, built our kitchens as separate rooms, closed off from the rest of the house to contain smells and noise, we can now aspire to 'open-plan' kitchen-dining areas and, in some cases, for there to be no intervening dividers between cooker and bed. So efficient is modern extraction, that it's now possible to conceive of the cooking 'fire' coming back into the same room in which the householder lives and sleeps.

The Deutsches Hygiene Museum was founded in Dresden in 1912 by Karl August Lingner, a local manufacturer of hygiene products. It was intended as a global centre for research into public health and medicine and organised travelling exhibitions that spread the latest research and innovations all over the word. One travelling exhibition in 1927 featured the latest in kitchen design and prominently advocated the use of hard, white surfaces: tile, enamel and the new lead-free gloss paints. This wasn't purely about sterile surfaces; it was also about light. Light meant health.

Old-style housing was dark. Glass was expensive, and windows meant cold and draughts. Gas lighting had extended the working day for many but, like candles, it was inefficient and produced soot and dust. Electric lighting brought a clean, bright future into the house and white surfaces enhanced the effect. If one were to walk from a Victorian kitchen into a modern one, perhaps the single most noticeable difference would be the light, not just the high-output overhead lighting we're all used to, but cleverly designed task lighting. It's probably the only place in the house you'll have workshop-quality light, focused directly on the work space, and above all the choice of colour palette and materials. Today, the kitchen isn't a dark, damp smelly place where hard physical work is done, but a light, bright shared living space with tones that reflect that feeling.

CHICKEN BRICK

LORD KNOWS, there are enough ancient traditions and traditional equipment still surviving in the modern kitchen, you'd think it wouldn't be necessary to make them up, but that, it seems, is what we've done.

In 1968 Habitat launched the Chicken Brick. It appears to have been invented by David Queensberry,* then a professor of ceramics at the Royal College of Art, and his partner Martin Hunt. Early versions were thrown on a wheel as normal pots and then, rather than having their lids sliced off, they were cut vertically with a wire. Possibly due to their phenomenal success, they were soon being mass-produced using less bucolic pressing techniques.

Although the design seems inspired by Mediterranean clay ovens and looks a bit rustic, nobody seems able to trace the 'chicken brick' back much before Sir Terence Conran decided to stock it. Even the name is odd. It doesn't look anything like a brick … it's a split pot. There is a famous old Tuscan recipe for *pollo al mattone* which is often called 'chicken under a brick', but it has nothing to do with roasting.[†]

In effect the chicken brick is just like any other enclosed roasting pan – well, maybe just a little more difficult to keep clean. But it served another purpose. Perhaps you couldn't afford an AGA in your tiny flat in Parsons Green. Perhaps you could never aspire to chicken roasted in the brick oven of your summer abode in Tuscany, but you could buy a tiny little rustic pot that fitted inside the wheezing, reeking, unaesthetic gas cooker in your shared kitchen and even bring it to the table to serve to your admiring friends. As a piece of authentic culinary history, the chicken brick is a sham, but as a piece of design in response to contemporary consumer needs, it's the sort of case study they'll be writing theses about for generations to come.

Like all essentially romantic items of kitchenware, the chicken brick soon built up its own substantial myths and a cult of starry-eyed adherents. True converts to the brick still cook whole meals in it and claim that the earthenware 'takes on the flavours', acquiring a sort of patination taste over years of loving care. For the rest of us, it will always remain an amusing place to keep the car keys.

---

* The 12th Marquess of Queensberry.

† The brick, in this case, is just used to weight down a spatchcocked chicken on a hot grill. Today most recipes suggest you wrap the brick in foil for cleanliness, which effectively denies the brick any chance to impart anything interesting to the meat at all.

CORKSCREW

A CORKSCREW designed specifically for the domestic kitchen is a surprisingly late innovation. In homes with servants, wine was deliberately kept away from the kitchen staff – partly because it needed special storage in a cellar, partly to avoid any chance of the staff being tempted by the demon drink. A butler might keep his own corkscrew for opening wine and in more modest households, it would have lived on the sideboard, a decorative object, for use by the master or mistress of the house when a bottle was 'brought up'.

Many writers from the 1930s onwards, including Kingsley Amis and Raymond Postgate, began to address the etiquette of drinking wine in unstaffed homes, but this was still targeted largely at the upper-class reader. Wine would still be bought from one's wine merchant or from a few specialist suppliers.

The real boom in home wine drinking took off in the 1970s. Until this point New World imports had consisted mainly of sweet or fortified Australian wines that could stand up to the rigours of transport; South African vineyards did the same, with their exports further impaired by embargoes and boycotts; and the North American wine industry had taken half a century to recover from the Prohibition era.

With wine now available through a growing network of off licenses and, later, supermarkets, wine was no longer something to keep in a cellar or rack and moved firmly into the kitchen. Chilled in the fridge, racked in the larder and easily picked up with the groceries, it became an 'everyday' rather than 'special occasion' drink.

The earliest T-shaped corkscrews were prone to going adrift through the cork and ripping it to pieces – enough of a mishap in a large cellar, but when opening a single bottle at home for a dinner party or as a special treat, a catastrophe in comparison. Other designs avoided this problem, some by using levers to assist in withdrawing or the highly successful 'Screwpull' type, which used a specially designed Teflon-coated helix, perfectly targeted at the cork by its plastic body. The most efficient corkscrew is the type pictured here (*opposite, top*), which uses a metal hook against the neck of the bottle to lever out the cork. This is popular with professional bottle openers and has thus become known as the 'waiter's friend'.*

---

* The 'waiter's friend' was invented in 1882 by Karl Wienke. The less common but equally useful 'butler's friend', on the other hand, comprised two sprung prongs that slide down either side of the cork without marking it – the cork could therefore be extracted and replaced without anyone noticing that the staff had been at the Château Margaux.

COFFEE MACHINES

WE HAVE HAD COFFEE SHOPS almost as long as we've had coffee and with them, the paraphernalia for consistent brewing in volume, but that didn't mean that people couldn't knock up a cup or two at home. It wasn't complicated to crush up a few beans, boil them up over the fire and either strain them through muslin or let the grounds settle, 'Turkish'-style.

Cona supplied many of the bulk coffee-making machines to Lyons Corner Houses and other mass catering establishments throughout the 1950s, but in 1960 they patented a vacuum coffee maker for home use. It was designed by Abram Games to look at home in the centre of a table – glass, chrome and with pointed handles in black thermoplastic. More importantly, it was fascinating to watch in action, like a classroom physics experiment. The coffee grounds were poured into the top container and water into the bottom where, heated by the flickering blue flame of a methylated spirit lamp, it boiled up through the central pipe and sprayed over the coffee.

Once all the water had boiled through, the flame was extinguished with a handy glass snuffer and the cooling air in the bottom vessel contracted, sucking the coffee back through the 'filter' of its own grounds. Even today, the Cona syphon is the brewing method of choice for coffee geeks all over the world. Sure, they claim it's the gentlest method for extracting flavour from spectacular beans and blends, but we know they are just as nerdily delighted by the theatre of it as their grandparents were.

It's important to distinguish between these 'syphon' coffee makers and the 'percolator'* patented in the USA in the 1880s. The percolator blows the boiling water up over the coffee, allows it to drip through under gravity and then, crucially, blows the coffee back up over the grounds. This repeated process extracts the maximum value from fewer grounds, producing a stronger and often more bitter brew. The heat of the process also drives off many of the volatile compounds in the coffee, creating a delicious smell at the expense of complexity of flavour. Until speciality coffee making went global in the 21st century, extra-strong 'perked jet-fuel' defined the American national taste.

Commercial espresso machines were first patented in the 1880s in Turin. They were designed to serve large numbers of workers, perhaps in a canteen or outside the factory gates, with consistently good coffee at high speed. This was achieved by pressurising water and steam to blow through a measured dose of coffee. The term 'espresso' puns on the notions of speed, pressure and 'expression' of flavours.

The 'moka pot' was designed by Luigi de Ponti for the Bialetti company in 1933 and brought espresso – or at least an acceptable simulacrum – into the domestic

---

* Though the percolator was patented in 1865 by James Nason of Franklin, Massachusetts, the original invention of the brewing method is attributed to Count Rumford, a physicist who is also credited with the invention of the first efficient cooking range in the 1790s and, surreally, thermal underwear.

kitchen. This was the peak of Italian Futurism, when design and fine art were influenced by speed and new technologies like aircraft and tanks. The big espresso machines were gleaming, steaming, chrome-trimmed hymns to the power of technology, but the stout little stove-top 'Dalek'* was an even truer symbol of the period. A cheap, mass-produced machine (*opposite*), it created an amphetamine-like fuel for the proletariat from steam and cast aluminium† alloy.

Water boils in the lower vessel, the steam creating enough pressure to force hot water up through the grounds. The coffee produced is viscous, oily and has a desireable 'crema', just like a commercial espresso, but is extracted at lower pressures. Sold as the 'Moka Express', this simple device – three castings and a couple of pieces of pressed stainless steel – brought foolproof espresso into millions of Italian homes. As the espresso craze spread around the world in the 1950s and 60s, the 'stovetop' moka pot went with it, an unchanged design classic that spoke of Italian sophistication and peerless industrial design. Even today, a 'Bialetti' on the stove imparts a certain cachet to the cook. The coffee it produces – concentrated, dark and a little sweet from lower pressure extraction – is instantly recognisable as 'Italian-style'.

The Moka Express was easy to copy and Renato Bialetti, who took over from his father Alfonso as the proprietor of the company in 1946, spent many years defending the original design. A trademark, a cartoon version of Alfonso Bialetti, was applied to every authentic pot. So serious was Bialetti's commitment to the design that when he died aged 93 in 2016, his children packed his ashes into a large size Moka Express before placing him in the family tomb alongside his wife.

The La Pavoni Europiccola – patented in 1961 and still in production today – was the first electrically heated, self-contained espresso machine designed for use in the home kitchen. The pressurising lever was familiar from a thousand espresso bars and a simple 'steam wand' coming off the boiler enabled milk to be frothed to make cappuccinos. For many years La Pavoni was a benchtop toy for serious Italophiles, but when the global coffee craze kicked off, it enjoyed a terrific surge in interest. From the late 1980s onwards, the Europiccola was used by stylists, photographers, film makers and ad men as visual shorthand for yuppie sophistication.

---

*   Bialettis are often nicknamed 'Daleks' in the UK after the *Doctor Who* foes. Deep in the realms of both science-fiction and coffee nerdery it has been separately suggested that the designers of both the stovetop and the alien were inspired by the costumes of Diaghilev's Ballets Russes.

†   Aluminium itself was a futuristic material, only extracted in commercially viable quantities in the late 19th century and entering more common use via aircraft manufacture in the First World War.

TOAST RACK

NOT EVERY NATION sees bread as something that comes in thin rectangular slices (see Bread bin, page 156) and not all cultures store loaves to the point where a few stale slices may be left over, but those countries that are fortunate enough to have tin-baked loaves know the true wonder of toast.

A slice of stale bread held in front of the fire until it crisps and browns and subsequently drenched in butter or dripping is one of the simplest imaginable domestic foods. It requires no kitchen and can be made in a tent, a dormitory, a nursery, a sickroom, in a gentleman's clubroom or student's lodgings and, perhaps as a result, is regarded with a Proustian level of happy nostalgia by entire nations.

Making toast is a solitary pursuit and thus every enthusiast still has their own way with it. You only need to look around any hotel dining room at breakfast, watching the different rituals at each table, to realise that this is a social minefield.

Personally, I am of the opinion that toast should be rushed from toaster to plate, as hot as it can be borne, and preferably hotter – in this way, huge amounts of butter can be melted into the bread's surface which is, self-evidently, the point. But there are others who stray from the true path.

Toast cannot be allowed to lie flat and unbuttered – on a serving plate for example – without becoming unappetisingly soggy,[*] and so the toast rack came into being. A toast rack stops the toast going soggy, keeps it crisp, but at the cost of heat, and it is here, as in everything British, that the element of class enters the picture. The workman at his brazier, the farm worker at his hearth or even the student with her electric toaster, can pop the hot stuff directly on to the plate and enjoy sublime toast without effort, while the aristocrat must have their toast, made by staff, brought to them over time and distance. The toast rack meant that the aristocracy could at least enjoy crisp toast ... albeit cold. The rack, though, became a badge of refinement.[†]

---

[*] I'm told there are people who actually like it this way, but they are mercifully few and can be safely dismissed as lunatics.

[†] In my own childhood I remember the toast rack being placed on the table, I remember my mother trying to get the hot toast into the rack, and the howling mob of offspring tearing it straight out again before it could cool.

THERMOMETER

THE EARLIEST STOVES and ovens had no refinement of temperature control at all. Victorian recipe books speak of cooking 'over a bright fire' or in a 'moderate' or 'low' oven, but otherwise left anything like measurement to the cook's own experience and judgement.

This was no doubt a reasonable way to instruct a cook who'd been doing the job for a lifetime, used to a repertoire of dishes and a consistent cooking range, but for the home cook such experience was harder won. Trying a new recipe could often result in expensive failure if you couldn't control and judge temperature in a repeatable and standardised way.

As electric oven design was refined, they were made more finely controllable with a variable resistance or 'rheostat'; an equivalent heat controller, the 'Regulo', was developed for gas. The manufacturers of both appliances made great efforts to publish cookbooks that used their temperature setting systems and, to this day, most recipes are published with centigrade and/or fahrenheit temperatures for electric and 'gas marks' for gas cookers.

What's important to understand for the keen cook, however, is that these are not absolute temperatures but estimated markings on the controls of the appliance. Actual measurement shows most cookers to be inaccurate by up to 20°C (68°F) in either direction and often inconsistent.

Accurate thermometers have been available to cooks since they were invented by Daniel Fahrenheit in 1714, but unfortunately, though accurate, they were made of delicate glass and mercury. 'Spirit' thermometers, containing a red-dyed alcohol instead of toxic mercury, were adopted in kitchens but were woefully inaccurate. The third type – which relied on the action of heat on a bimetallic strip to turn a needle on a dial – was even less accurate, though, in its favour, it was robust enough to place inside the oven.

It's remarkable that only in very recent years have oven manufacturers managed to install an electronic thermometer that reads the actual temperature inside the oven.

Perhaps one of the most exciting and useful developments in modern cookery has been the electronic probe thermometer. This enables the cook to test the temperature inside the food for the first time – so even the most inexperienced cook can tell precisely when food is safely cooked throughout. Though some still regard the probe as complicated, it's important enough in commercial food service that you'll see everyone from school dinner ladies to the kid with acne and a paper hat at your local burger franchise probing all the food before serving.

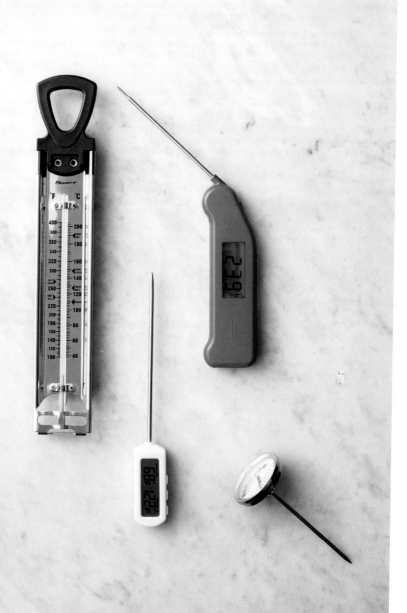

BUTTER DISH

BUTTER VARIES A GREAT DEAL depending on where it's made. Traditionally it was a way of preserving milk so that the fat was separated from the more perishable portion and often fermented to increase its life.*

Many European butters are very substantially fermented, and ghee – used as a cooking fat across South Asia – is so completely fermented it can survive for months unrefrigerated. In the UK and United States, most customers seem to dislike the slightly funky flavour of fermentation and so unfermented butter, sometimes enriched with fresh cream, is more the norm.

Unfermented butters must be refrigerated if they're not to go cheesy or rancid, but this, of course, makes them solid and extremely difficult to spread.

The butter dish is intended to ameliorate the problem. It's designed to protect a block of butter from air and dirt so it can be stored outside the fridge. In kitchens with traditional larders this meant the butter could stay at a reasonably stable temperature, lower than that of the kitchen but higher than the fridge, but in modern kitchens things are more difficult. Today, so much of our food requires refrigeration that we own large, rather cold, fridges to preserve it for longer. Fewer people have larders and modern, creamy, unfermented butter doesn't last as long at room temperature.

Many families will have interminable arguments about whether the butter dish lives inside or outside the fridge and in response, butter manufacturers increasingly offer 'butter' that's combined with vegetable fats and oils so it can 'spread straight from the fridge'.

Butter itself is under constant attack from the health lobby, so it seems unlikely that the butter dish will last another generation.

---

* 'Bog butter' is occasionally turned up on architectural digs in Ireland. A highly fermented, high fat content butter, packed into barrels and buried in the damp, anaerobic environment of a peat bog, it can remain edible for centuries.

SAUCE BOAT

THE SAUCE BOAT, a separate shallow jug for serving, is a hangover from the aristocratic table. Pouring the sauce to the taste of the individual diner is thought to have become fashionable in the French court during the 17th century and, as with many of the refinements in taste of the period, migrated quickly to the courts of Europe and the tables of the aspiring middle classes.

Sauce boats of various kinds have stayed in use all around the world, but it is in the UK where two national 'sauces' have made the vessel a regular and ubiquitous part of the place setting. Talleyrand is alleged to have made the observation:

England has three sauces and three hundred and sixty religions,
whereas France has three religions and three hundred and sixty sauces.

… which is quite possibly true. What he was incapable of comprehending is that we don't need sauces in England because we have gravy. Proper gravy, not brown gunge made from powder, is a complex creation that, when done well, balances all the available flavour sensations in the mouth while elegantly complementing the meat. It brings the plate into harmony like a talented choirmaster and makes the soul soar. Gravy is better than any sauce and, therefore, is worthy of its own vessel – a grail, if you will – with which it can be served at even the humblest of tables. This is the *gravy boat*.

Gravy doesn't really have a recipe and is made by stretching the available juices after the meat is cooked. At a Sunday Roast or Christmas dinner, the meat is not put onto the plates until it's been taken to the table, displayed and carved. The gravy needs somewhere to sit before it is properly and fairly shared from the boat.

It would be hard to imagine a single item that better sums up Britishness – the thrift and fairness, the ceremony and the class-consciousness – than the gravy boat. In a British family, the sauce boat takes on an extra, potent ritual significance when you remember that we also use it to serve custard.

ICE CREAM SCOOP

FOR MOST OF CULINARY HISTORY, ice has been a luxury. Initially it was harvested during the winter months and could be stored in insulated icehouses – but this was only really feasible in enormous quantities. The larger the quantity of ice stored, the slower it will be diminished by melting; thus, a giant insulated, underground ice-store could hold thousands of tons through a whole summer while a small insulated box of ice at home would melt in hours.

Until the 1930s ice cream manufacturers used and stored enough ice to make their product and sold it from insulated carts that could be recharged with enough ice to last for hours. The serving only had to last long enough to be consumed outdoors,* but the unique economics of the ice trade meant that ice cream was either a manufactured treat, bought on the street, or the impossibly luxurious product of a grand restaurant or palace kitchen.

It was only with the arrival of home refrigerators – most of which had a freezer section small enough to hold an ice tray – that ice cream manufacturers could sell to householders to keep. In fact, with few shops having display freezers, many companies would sell direct from their retail trucks – often in a cardboard wrapped 'brick' shape that could slip easily into the tiny freezer compartment in place of an ice tray. Domestic kitchens only needed ice cream scoops once home freezers were big enough to hold large tubs of ice cream. This particular scoop is the neat design popular in American diners. The aluminium casting is an excellent conductor of heat so, after holding for only a few seconds, the heat of the user's hand is transmitted to the bowl where it warms and frees a perfect ball of ice cream.

---

* Early ice cream vendors – often Italians – would site their kitchens close to ice storage facilities. The ice cream was served in small chilled glass or metal cups which the customer would return immediately they'd finished eating – the ice cream clearly wasn't designed to survive any longer than the time it took to eat standing next to the cart. The salesmen attracted customers by shouting 'ecco un poco' or 'here's a little bit', which was quickly corrupted into 'hokey-pokey' – this became the slang term for ice cream.

TIERED CAKE/SANDWICH PLATE

MOST FOOD IS, by necessity, cooked and served horizontally, laid in pans or cooking trays and then served on flatware. Liquids naturally find their own level so sauces or gravies spread out across the bottom of the plate. Raising things higher on the dinner table seems to be a shorthand for elegance. Tall-stemmed wine glasses look more celebratory than the sort of stumpy tumbler from which you might neck your everyday *vin de table*. Meat in a normal meal is sliced or cubed and arranged flat on a plate, whereas, at an 'important' meal, it arrives 'whole' in a joint to be carved – a fork stuck in the top for extra pizzazz. Perhaps the single most conspicuously celebratory food most of us will ever experience is the wedding cake, multi-tiered and topped with flowers or effigies.

The tiered plate brings such elegance to more domestic gatherings. Loaded with canapés it becomes the central display of a cocktail party, laden with cakes it forms the root and core of the cakeshop 'tea' and, perhaps most significantly, it's the essential object upon which 'high tea' is constructed.

The tiered cake plate was such a powerful symbol of social aspiration and refinement that it's now remembered with fond nostalgia. Restaurants and tearooms wanting a 'vintage' feel serve gorgeous selections of food in tiny servings on tiered stands. I know from daily experience that it is still impossible to place the towering plate on the table without a subconscious flourish.*

---

* I am fortunate enough to own a tea shop in Cambridge where waitresses daily serve formal teas with high-tiered cake-plates. The flourish is alive and well.

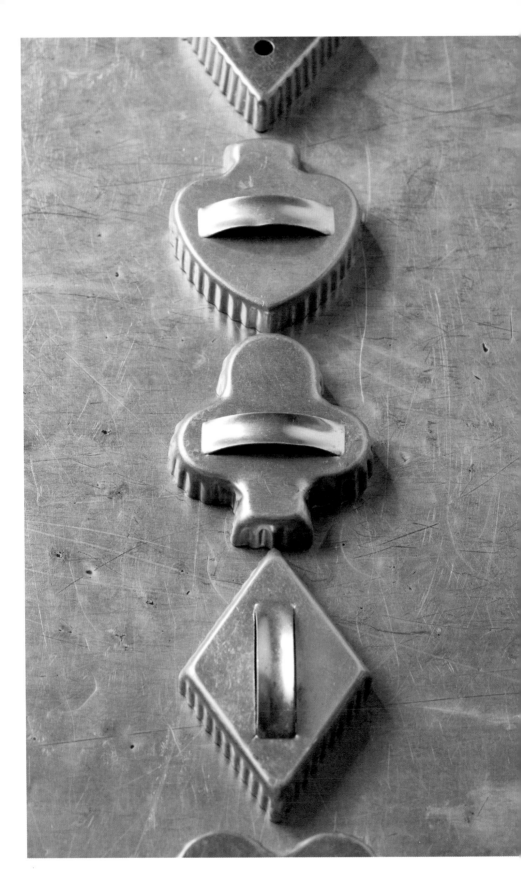

'BRIDGE' SANDWICH CUTTERS

IT'S EASY TO THINK that the prime purpose of domestic cookery is feeding the family, but because food is shared socially, it has a second function: social display. The great feasts and banquets of royalty and aristocracy are amply recorded and we know that throughout history, it was common to serve enormous surfeits of rare and costly foods as a statement of power and superiority – conspicuous consumption in both senses of the word – or in an act of hospitable fealty.

Medieval feasts could be outrageously spectacular, but eating as political display probably reached its peak in the early 19th century. Antonin Carême, a pastry chef of international renown, famously created monumental pastry and sugarwork centre-pieces for the likes of Talleyrand, Napoleon, the Prince Regent and James Rothschild. These creations, sometimes several metres high, were never intended to be eaten … just admired.

Although this kind of culinary architecture was beyond the scope of home cooks, most social climbers were no less aware of the power of food and dining in manoeu-vring their way ahead of the Joneses. Even the very earliest cookbooks are written as much as guides to impressing one's guests as they are instructions for feeding the family. And even the simplest of dishes could be turned, in some small way, into displays of refinement.

At the turn of the 20th century a craze for playing bridge developed which, perhaps in the absence of other forms of home entertainment, rapidly became a popular social event in countries all over the world. A 1940 survey* found that it was played in 44 per cent of US homes. A hostess would be sternly judged on the refresh-ments she provided during the games, particularly in those cultures looking to re-es-tablish social hierarchy after the troubling egalitarianism of war.

These simple cutters in the shape of the card suits could be pushed into thinly cut sandwiches, instantly turning a quick and easy snack into a far more elegant 'canapé' of sorts.

---

* By the American Association of Playing Card Manufacturers.

OVENPROOF GLASS

DON'T TRY THIS AT HOME, but if you pour boiling water into a wine glass, it will shatter. The phenomenon is known as 'thermal shock' and it occurs when different parts of a material expand at different rates and can't quite take the stresses imposed. Borosilicate glass, discovered at the end of the 19th century, is resistant to expansion and thermal shock. It was originally used in lab equipment and optics* but was soon adapted for culinary use. In 1915 the Corning company in the USA created their own proprietary borosilicate, which they introduced under the trade name PYREX™. PYREX was wonderful stuff. Cooks could now watch their food cooking. You could take a measuring jug, see through it and fill it with boiling liquid. Better still, glass somehow felt just as right on the dining table as it suddenly did in the kitchen. A casserole cooked in PYREX didn't have to be laboriously decanted into a serving dish where it would quickly congeal. Instead the whole lot could be brought straight to the table and served hot.

PYREX is rarely if ever seen in professional kitchens. It's unsuitable for the gentle ministrations of the professional dishwasher, and glass is still seen as a danger in mass catering environments. It has, though, remained a fixture in the domestic setting through a century of fickle fashion.

I admit that I love the clean 'laboratory' associations of clear, simple PYREX, as did home cooks in the first half of the 20th century and many of the modernist kitchen designers,† but in later years this was considered perhaps too purely functional for the housewife. In the 1960s they began making the glass opaque and overprinting patterns to make the material look more like a traditional ceramic. For the English market, the 'Tally Ho' range featured transfers of hunting scenes and in later years, in a sort of circular frenzy of unintentional post-modernism, they even produced a range that was coloured and textured to look like rough earthenware.

---

* Discovered in 1893 by Otto Schott of German company Schott AG. The first borosilicate glass lab products were sold as 'Duran'.

† Wagenfeld egg coddler (see page 106).

ON
THE FUTURE
KITCHEN

URING THE SURPRISINGLY short period of history that ordinary people have had kitchens, they have evolved rapidly, but with the speed of technological and social change now overtaking us it seems that our comfortable perception of the kitchen is under assault from all directions. Many of the large appliance companies have either launched 'connected' kitchen equipment or piloted it in 'kitchen of the future' experiments. Connecting ovens, fridges and coffee machines to home networks is a vital part of the 'Internet of things'.

It's already possible to read the barcode on packaged food and have the cooking settings downloaded to your oven. That unique barcoded product number also means that fridges can 'know' when you're running low on food and, with your permission, reorder from an online supplier. RFID technology – that's the disposable little 'chip' in your contactless cash card – is now so cheap and easy that soon your kitchen will 'read' all the information it needs from the packaging without the need for a scan. In effect the kitchen will 'communicate' with your groceries. It is true that we're still needed to take things out of their delivery bags and put them on the shelves, or to load ingredients into, say, a breadmaker, but with the technologies of 'ready meals' improving daily, the number of steps between delivery and plate that actually require a living, human 'cook' is going to be reduced to the minimum.

We have also changed how we choose what we eat. The likelihood of three family members actually sharing dietary preferences is rare enough; with any larger family it's approaching 'statistically impossible'. Between allergies, intolerances, preferences and various forms of exclusion diet, we have come to accept that eating, even in the most important of communal dining spaces, is completely personal. In a world where 'choice' is seen as more of a right than a privilege, the notion of 'eat what's on your plate and be glad of it' seems horribly Victorian.

With more food preparation taking place outside the home, things are better portioned than when cooking from scratch. Food increasingly comes in controlled portions so that even if the family can be persuaded to sit down together, they may not be 'sharing' a meal in the accepted sense. If Mum wants the curry and Dad wants the salad and the kids want vegan Mexican, everybody can have exactly what they want at the same time. For those with knowledge of the real history of the family kitchen this could be interpreted as a return to the very earliest way that urban families ate at home – reheating food bought at cookshops, with father, mother and various children eating entirely separate foods.

Perhaps the most radical change will be the huge and rapid success of new models of distributed delivery. Freelance drivers picking up orders from restaurant kitchens and delivering hot to the table mean that any need to cook at home is finally removed.

So with the technologies available to us, the pressures of modern family life and the constant pressure marketing of ever simpler 'meal solutions' in and out of the home, does the kitchen have a future? Can the home kitchen survive if we don't cook in it? I believe it does. The question, though, is 'what will it be for?'

The domestic kitchen evolved as a space for food preparation, it occurred as services and utilities became available and equipment and utensils were invented to suit a developing need. As time has passed, the drive for efficiency and 'labour saving' – and latterly the highly marketed notion of 'convenience' – have meant that the amounts of cooking that take place there have reduced and yet, at the same time, the importance of the kitchen as a social facility for the family, an almost sacred space in which to play out the vital rituals that hold a family together, has increased.

For a while back there, it felt like the functional intentions of those first pioneers were being undermined by false nostalgia for a romanticised 'family kitchen' – happy kids around the stripped pine table and mum stirring porridge at the AGA – but today, with the cooking function less to the fore, many people see the main purpose of the kitchen as a family room in which the remaining rituals, cooking and eating, *sometimes* take place. The modern kitchen has continued to evolve as ever it did, never straying from functionality... It's just that its *function* has changed.

ACKNOWLEDGEMENTS

With every book I write I become more firmly convinced that this is a totally collaborative business. Once again, *The Modern Kitchen* couldn't have happened without the instinctive visual brilliance and utter professionalism of designer Will Webb and the inspiration and overall guiding genius of my publisher Sarah Lavelle. It's a privilege to be in a team with them and an injustice that their names aren't on the cover.

Helen Lewis applied her phenomenal experience as creative director at exactly the right moments.

Photographer Sarah Hogan and stylist Alex Breeze pulled things together in the studio, giving a coherent visual look to essentially incoherent objects. Assistant Sophie Bronze also gave us on-the-spot Photoshop work every bit as outstanding as her gluten-free baked goods.

Special thanks to Chris Terry, whose work on test shoots helped us to understand the scope that this book could eventually have.

At Quadrille, thank you to Nikolaus Ginelli, who ensured this book was made to the highest production standards, and Emma Marijewycz, Fiona C. Smith, Ella Sparrenius-Waters, Laura Willis, Caroline Proud and Margaux Durigon who, among others, will get *The Modern Kitchen* into your hands.

Thanks to Dr Annie Gray for selfless historical assistance, responding day or night to texted requests for information, and to Professor Keith Brown and Professor Gillian Brown for the generous loan of utensils.

Thank you, Sandy Grant – it's a special kind of CEO who will personally go out and buy props – and thanks to Penny Rankin for an authentically battered peeler.

Thanks to Special Agent Tim.

Thanks, as always, to Alison and Liberty for tolerating my career decisions.

INDEX

Page numbers in *italics* refer to illustrations

Publishing Director: Sarah Lavelle
Creative Director: Helen Lewis
Designer: Will Webb
Photographer: Sarah Hogan
Prop Stylist: Alexander Breeze
Copy Editing: Jinny Johnson and Jennifer Latham
Production: Vincent Smith and Nikolaus Ginelli

First published in 2017 by Quadrille, an imprint of Hardie Grant Publishing

Quadrille
52–54 Southwark Street
London SE1 1UN
www.quadrille.com

The author and publishers wish to thank David Mellor (www.davidmellordesign.com)
for lending from their great range of kitchenware, as well as Sous Chef (www.souschef.
co.uk) for the loan of specialist cooking tools. Thanks also to Lakeland (www.lakeland.
co.uk) for providing a slow cooker and dabba for photography.

Thanks also to Alessi, Robot-Coupe, KitchenAid and Prestige for their kind co-operation
in lending products that were photographed for this book.

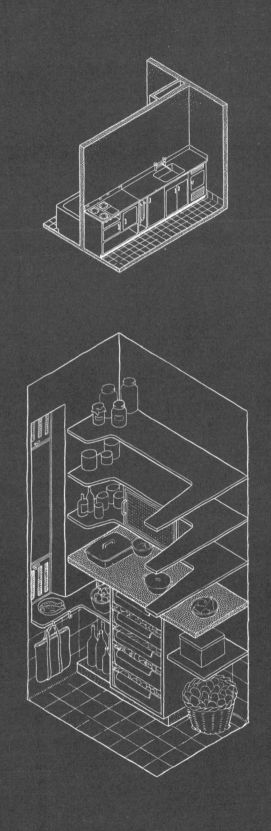